PHOTOGRAPHY WITH PETE:
NATURAL HORIZONS

A collection of over 25 photographs from the United States and Europe, focusing on what I felt to be breath-taking images from nature incorporating a horizon or skyline.

Peter Monego

From the streams near Thomas Jefferson's former home in Monticello, Virginia,

To the Vermont shoreline off of Lake Champlain.

To Hull and back, Hull, Massachusetts that is…

From the not-so-Red Light District of Amsterdam during the day,

To the London Bridge that wobbles but doesn't fall.

Cancun...enough said.

Even some of my old Black and White photos from High School….

Enjoy!

-Pete

SUNRISE I, II AND III

FRAMINGHAM, MASSACHUSETTS, USA

SUNSET I, II AND III

NARRAGANSET BEACH, HULL, MASSACHUSETTS, USA

MORNING I, II AND III

DOVER, MASSACHUSETTS, USA

WALLASTON I, II, III, IV AND V

QUINCY, MASSACHUSETTS, USA

WACHUSETT I, II, III and IV

WORCESTER, MA

6 LOCATION-SHOOTS OUTSIDE OF MASSACHUSETTS:

NIAGARA FALLS, NY, USA

ROUTE 80, PA, USA

LAKE CHAMPLAIN, VERMONT, USA

PUNTA NIZUC, CANCUN, MEXICO

THAMES RIVER, LONDON, ENGLAND

DE WALLEN, AMSTERDAM, NETHERLANDS

HIGH SCHOOL BLACK AND WHITES I, II, III, IV and V

DOVER, MASSACHUSETTS, USA

MONTICELLO, VIRGINIA, USA

SUNRISE I

FRAMINGHAM, MASSACHUSETTS, USA

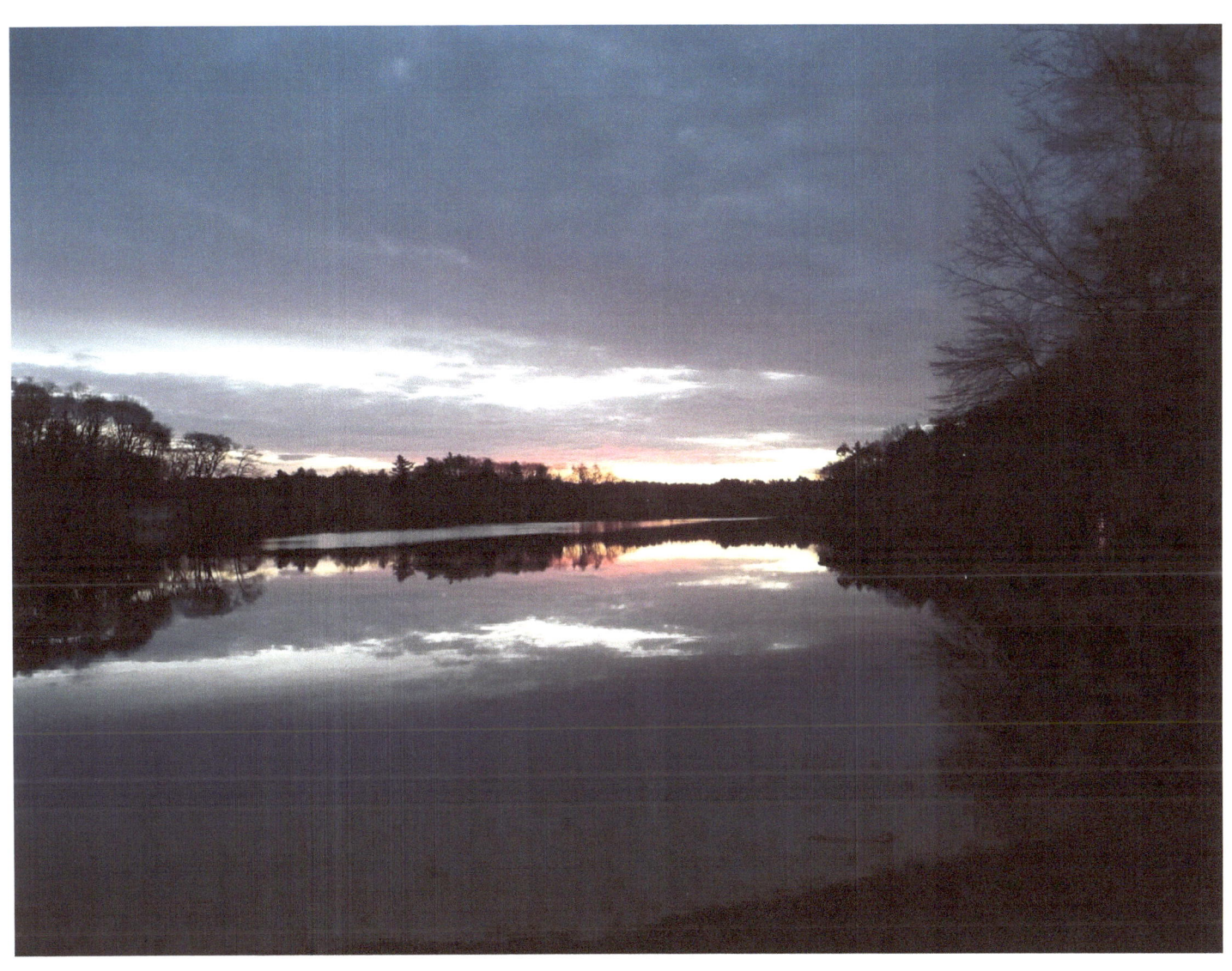

SUNRISE II

FRAMINGHAM, MASSACHUSETTS, USA

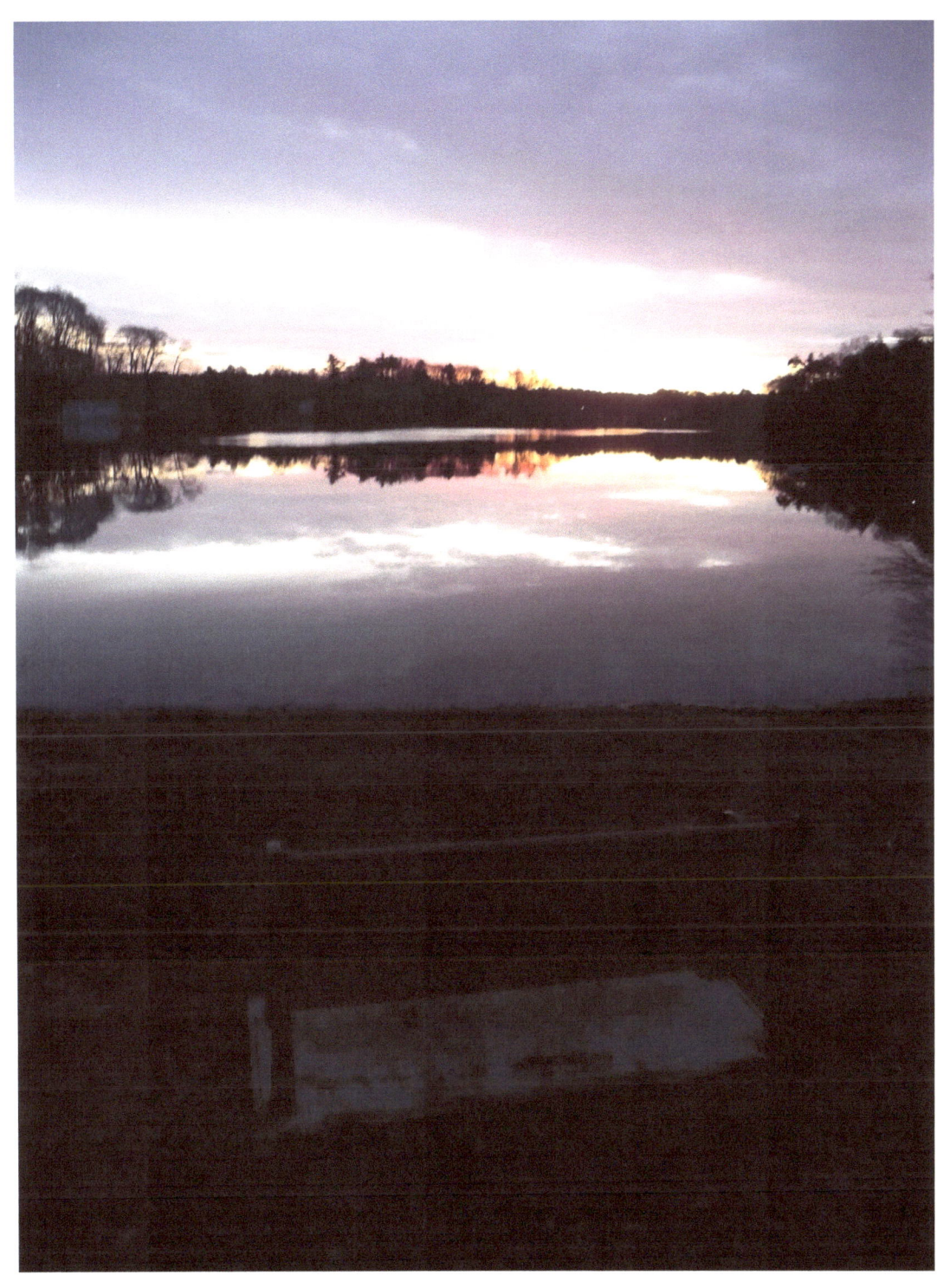

SUNRISE III

FRAMINGHAM, MASSACHUSETTS, USA

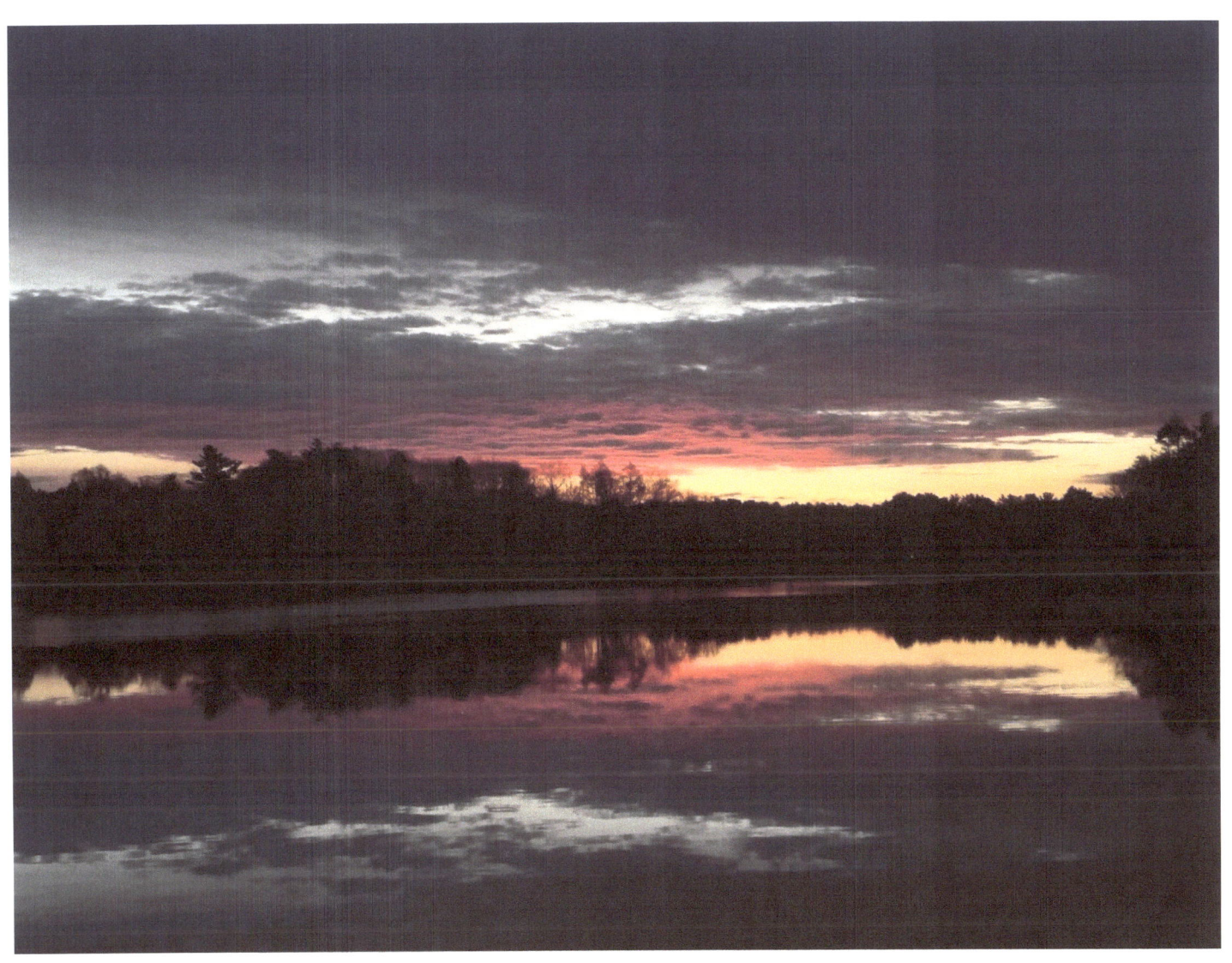

SUNSET I

NARRAGANSET BEACH

HULL, MASSACHUSETTS

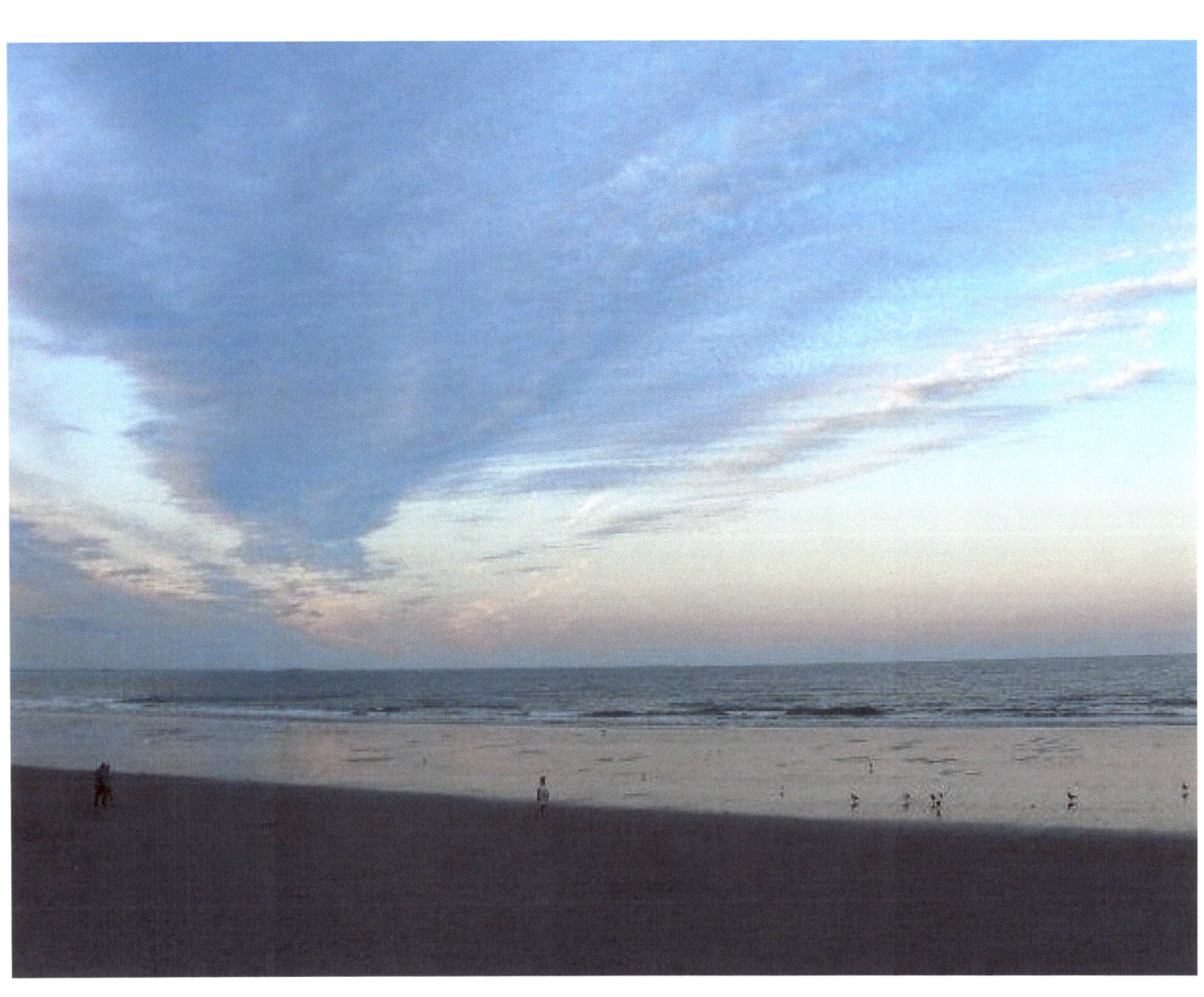

SUNSET II

NARRAGANSET BEACH

HULL, MASSACHUSETTS

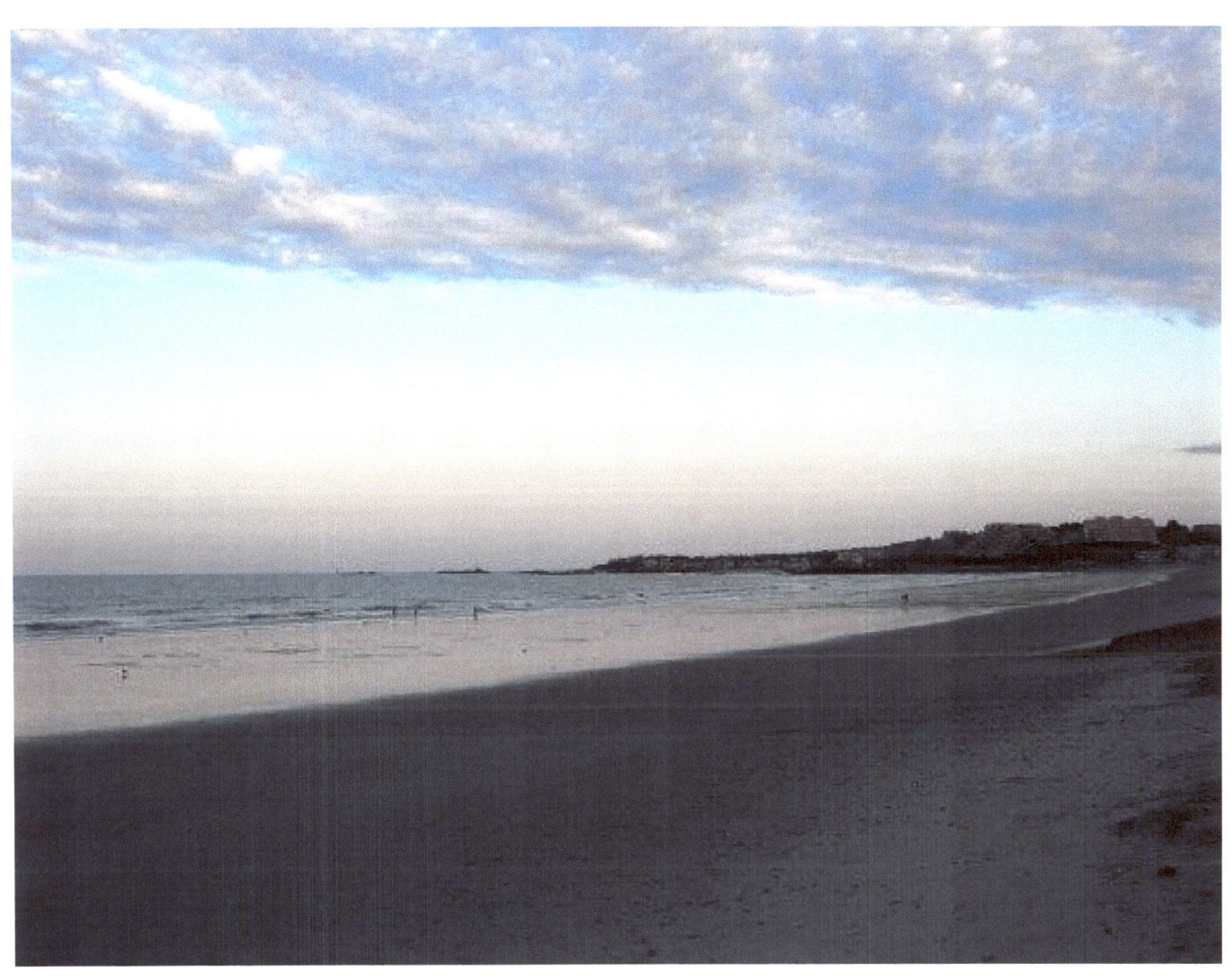

SUNSET III

NARRAGANSET BEACH

HULL, MASSACHUSETTS

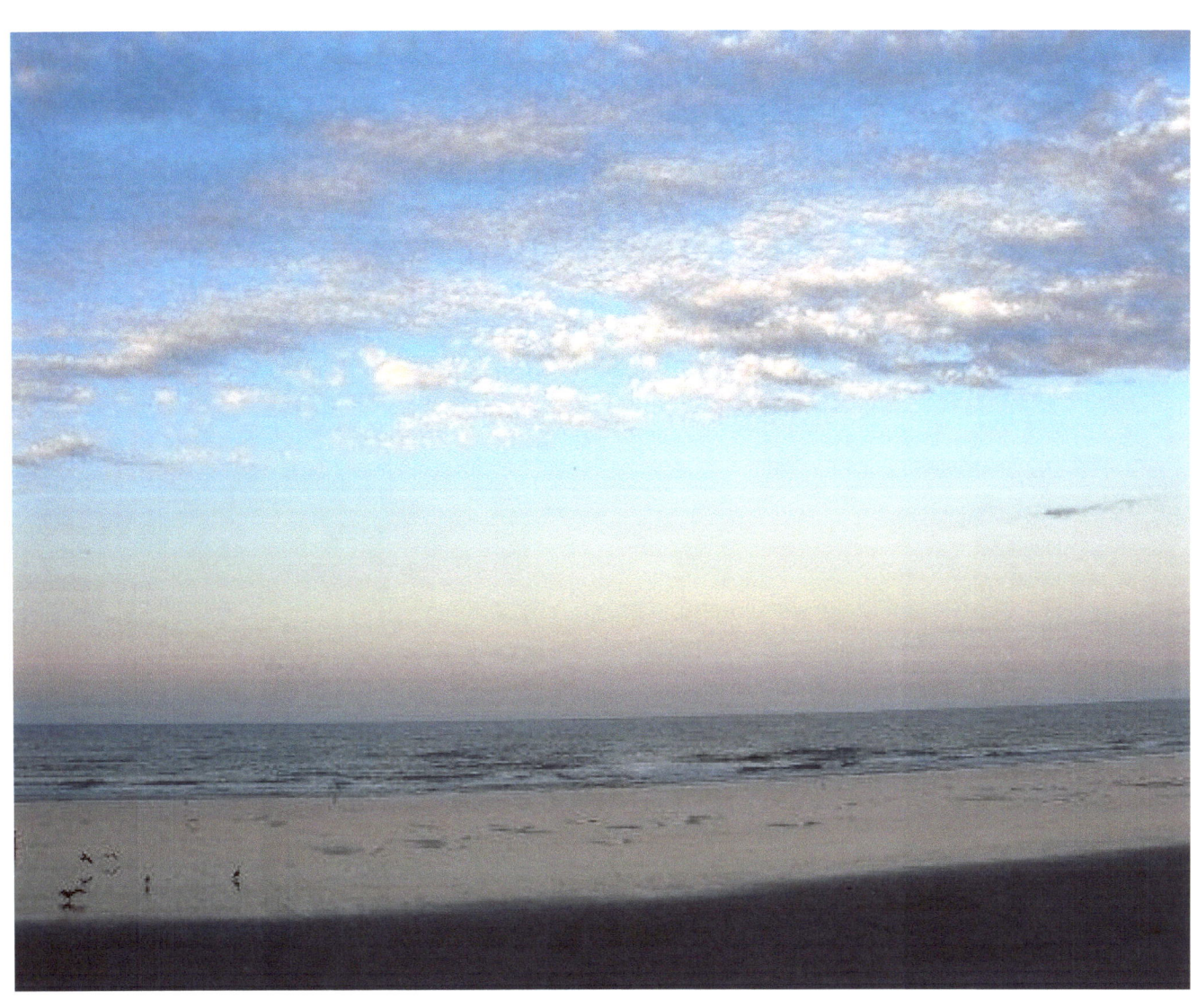

MORNING I

DOVER, MASSACHUSETTS, USA

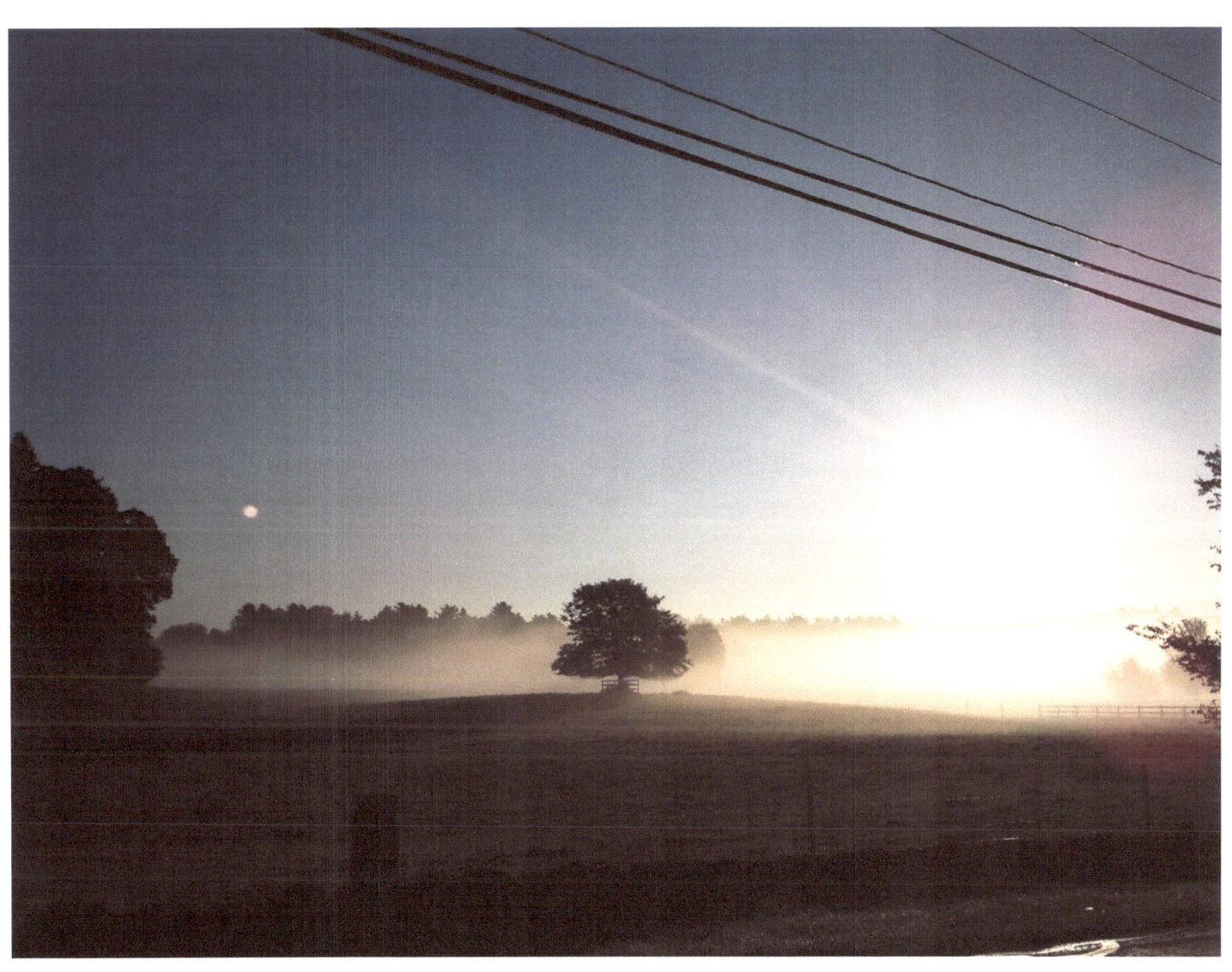

MORNING II

DOVER, MASSACHUSETTS, USA

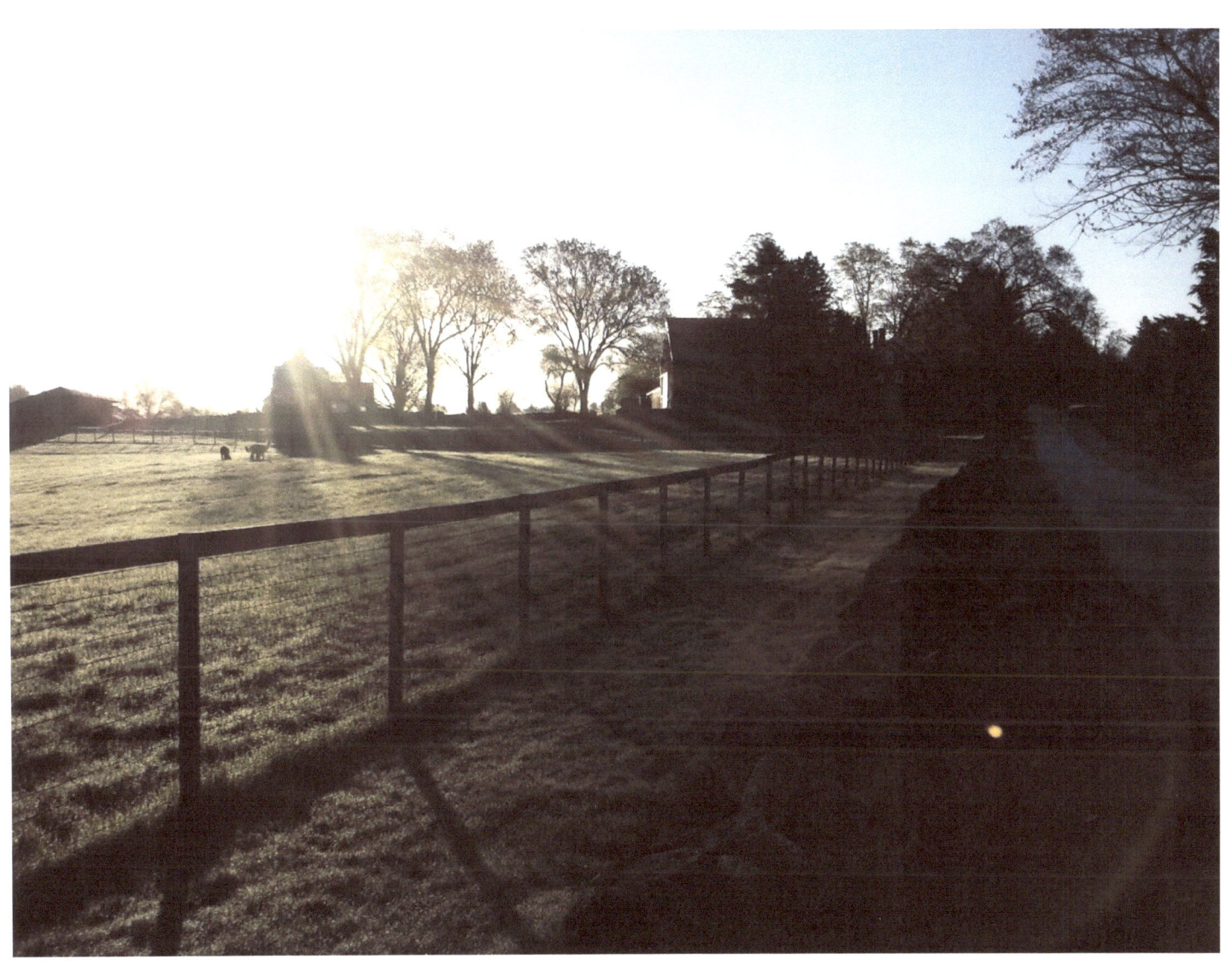

MORNING III

DOVER, MASSACHUSETTS, USA

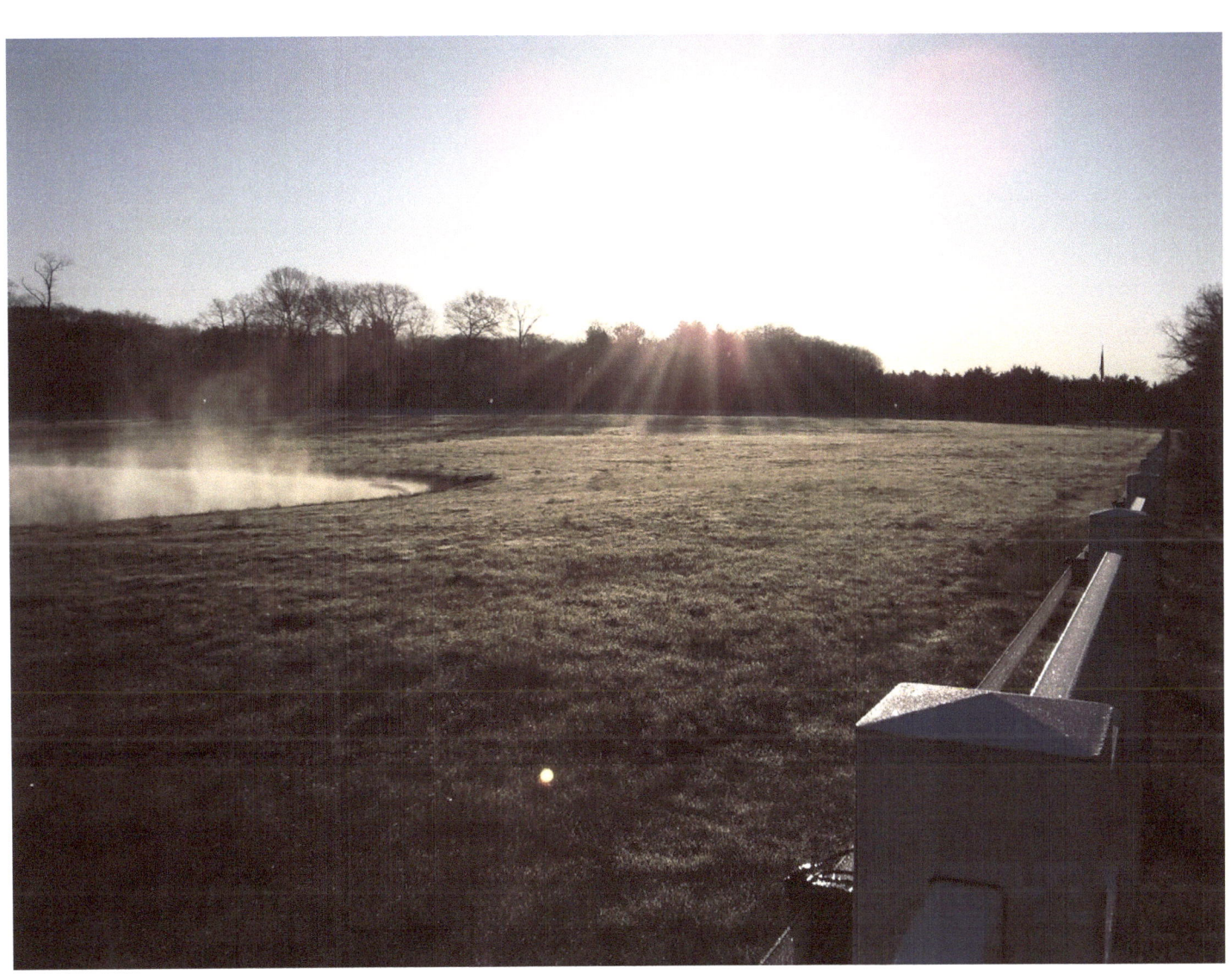

WALLASTON I

QUINCY, MASSACHUSETTS, USA

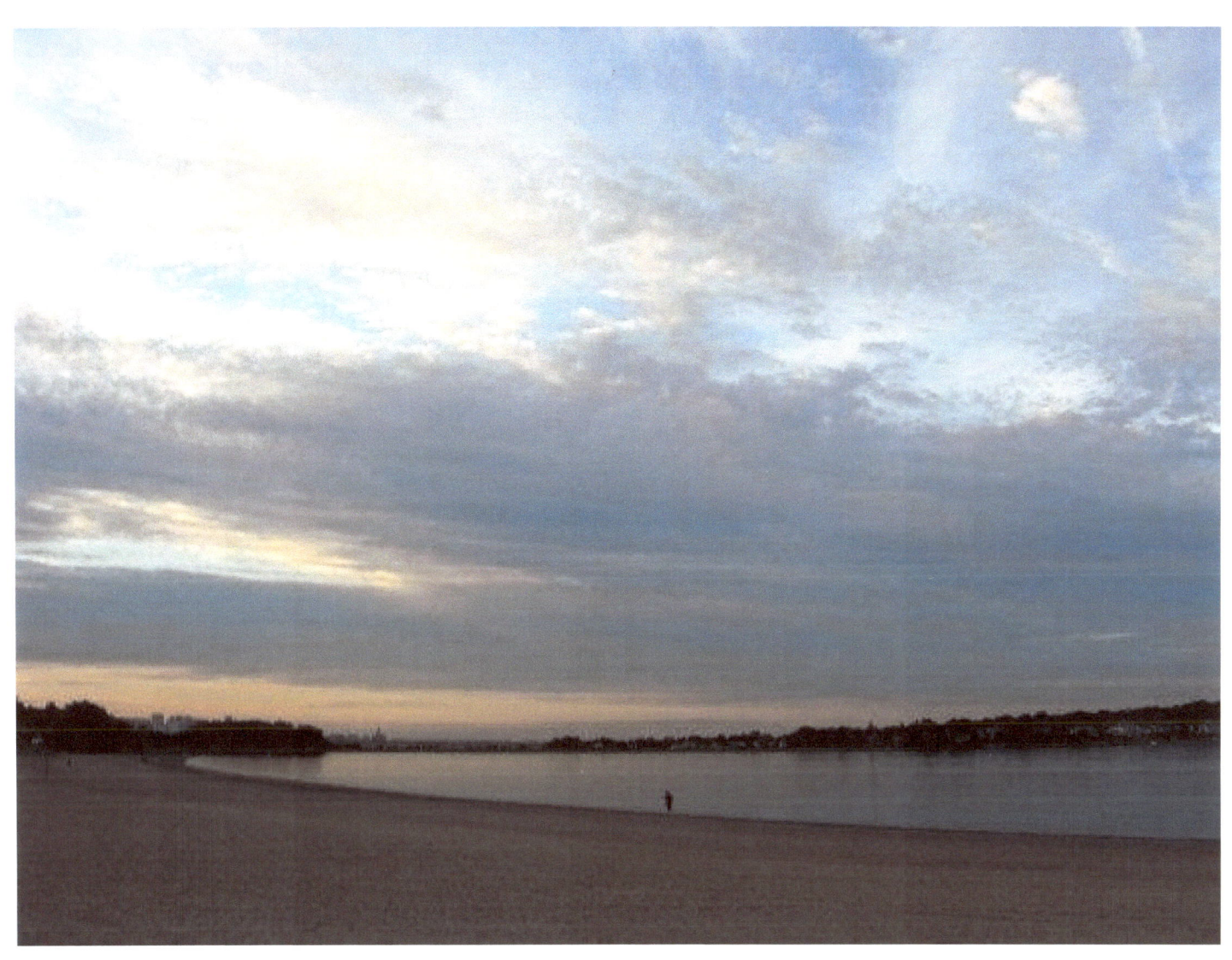

WALLASTON II

QUINCY, MASSACHUSETTS, US

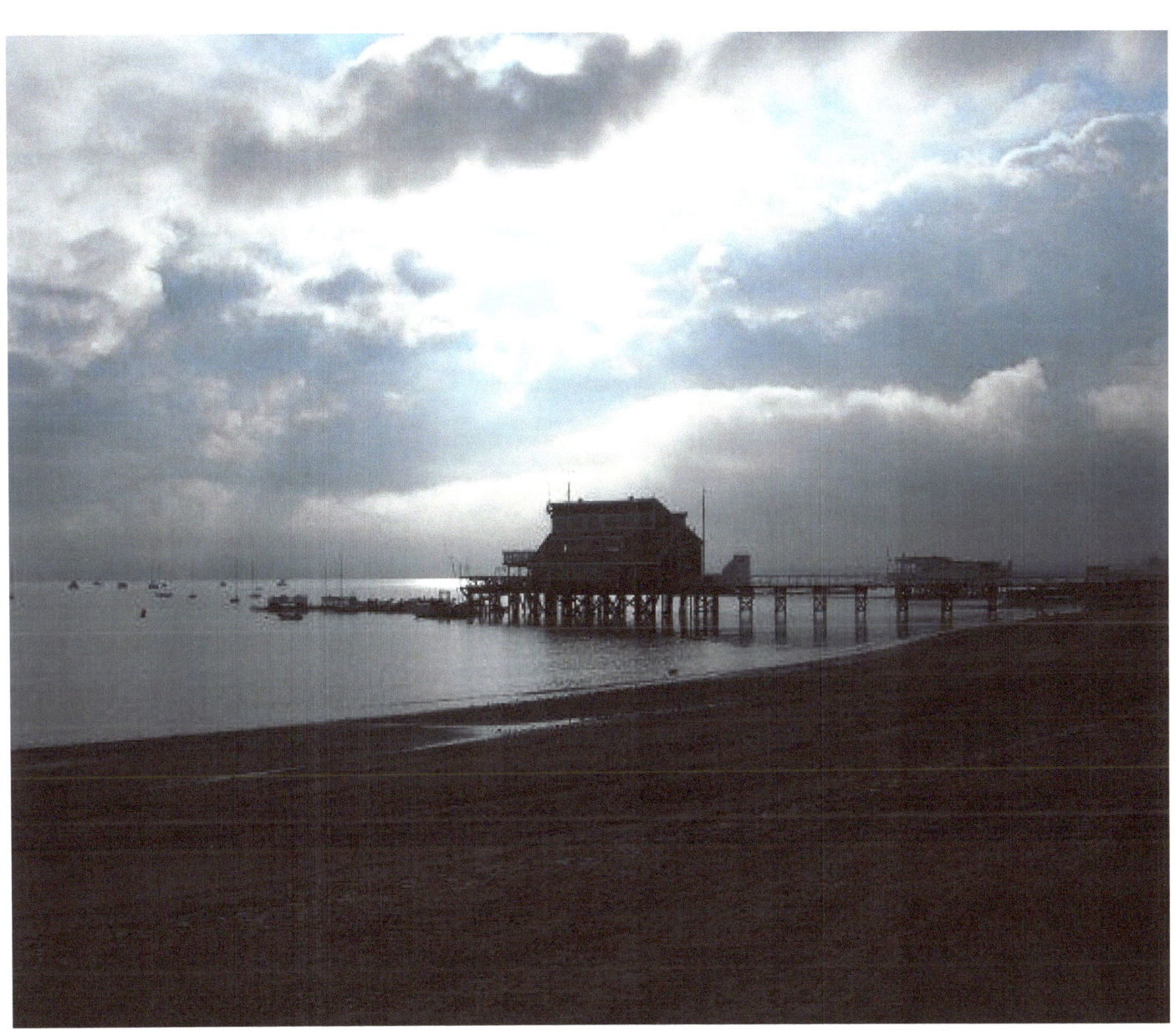

WALLASTON III

QUINCY, MASSACHUSETTS, USA

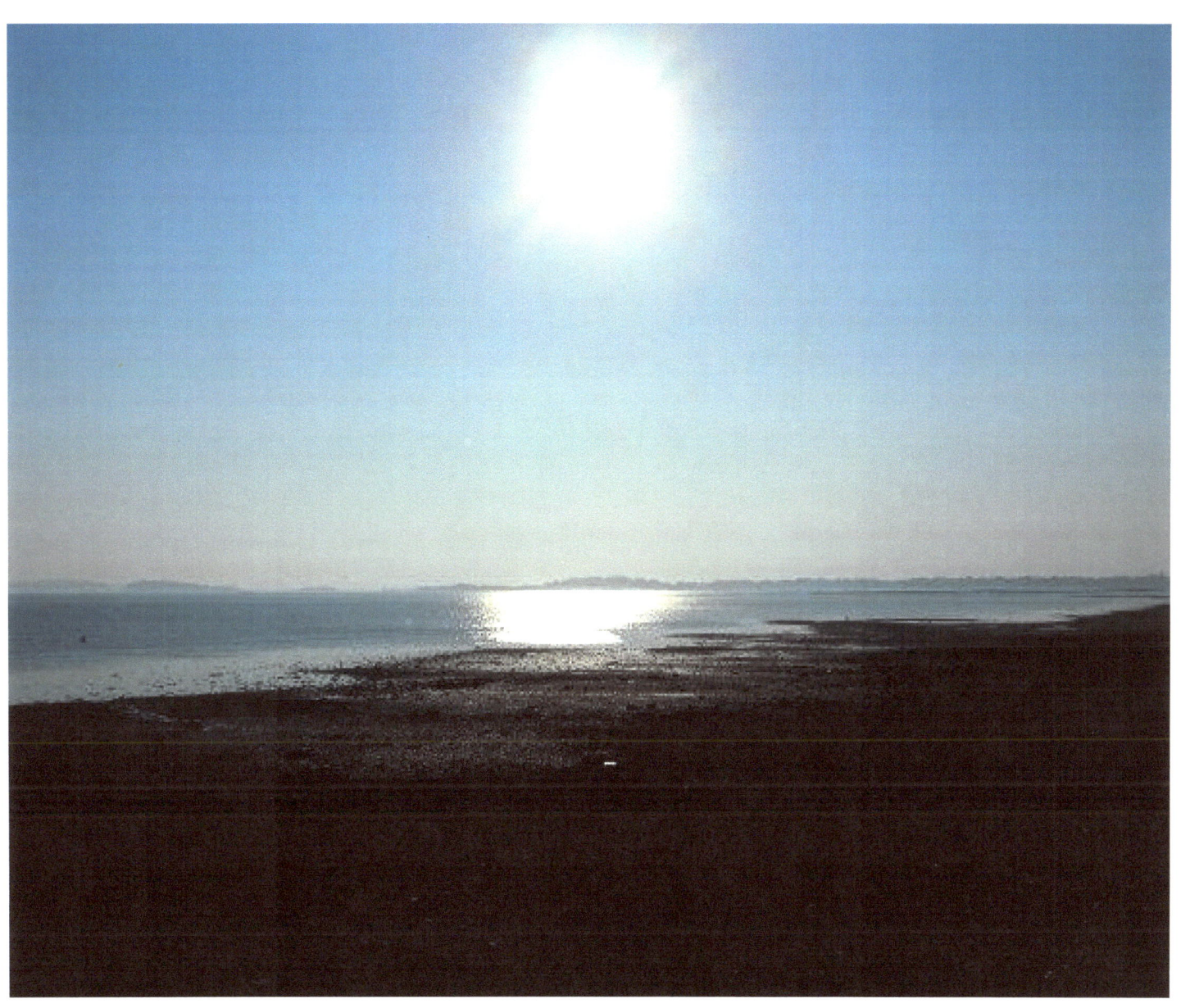

WALLASTON IV

QUINCY, MASSACHUSETTS, USA

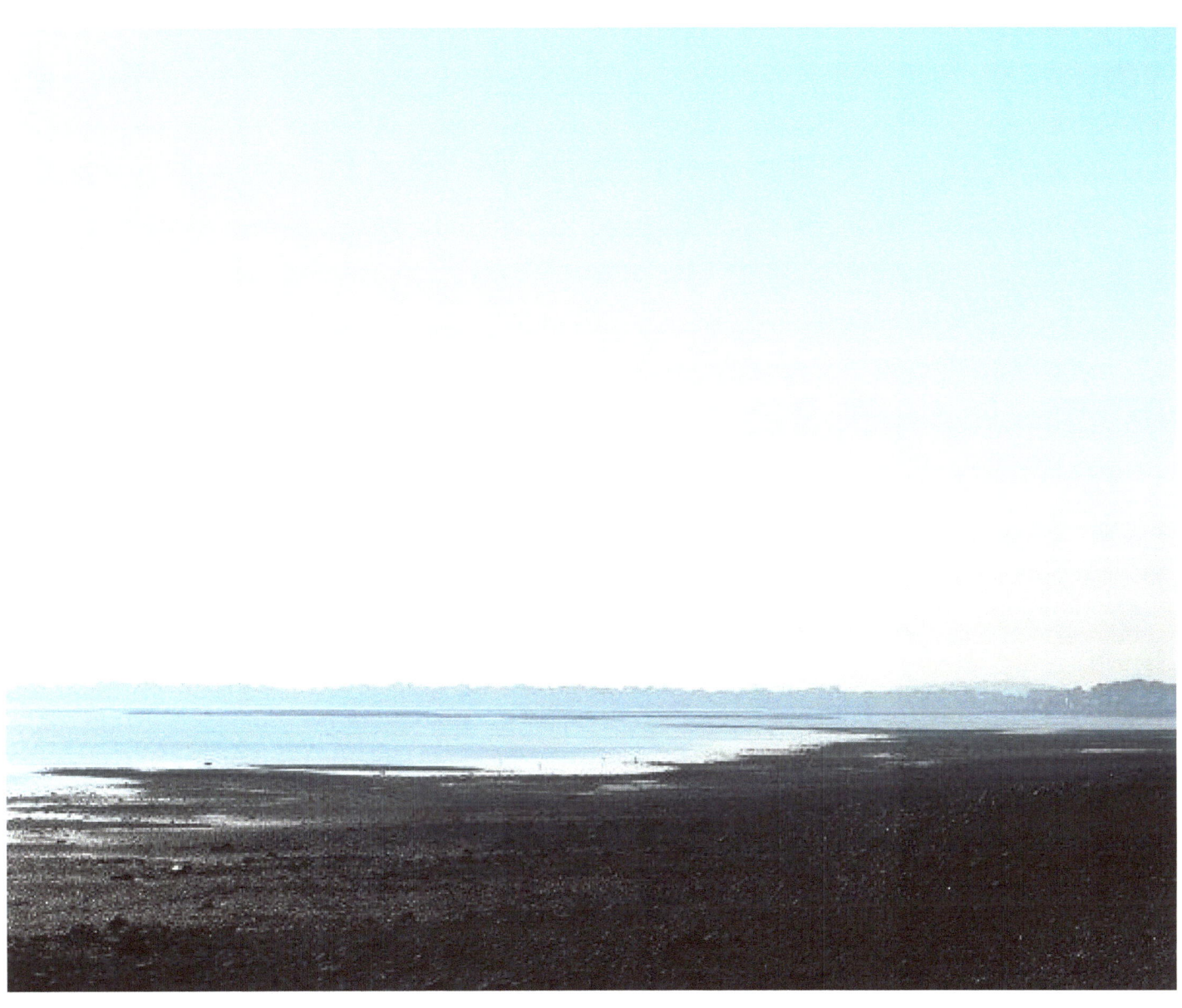

WALLASTON V

QUINCY, MASSACHUSETTS, USA

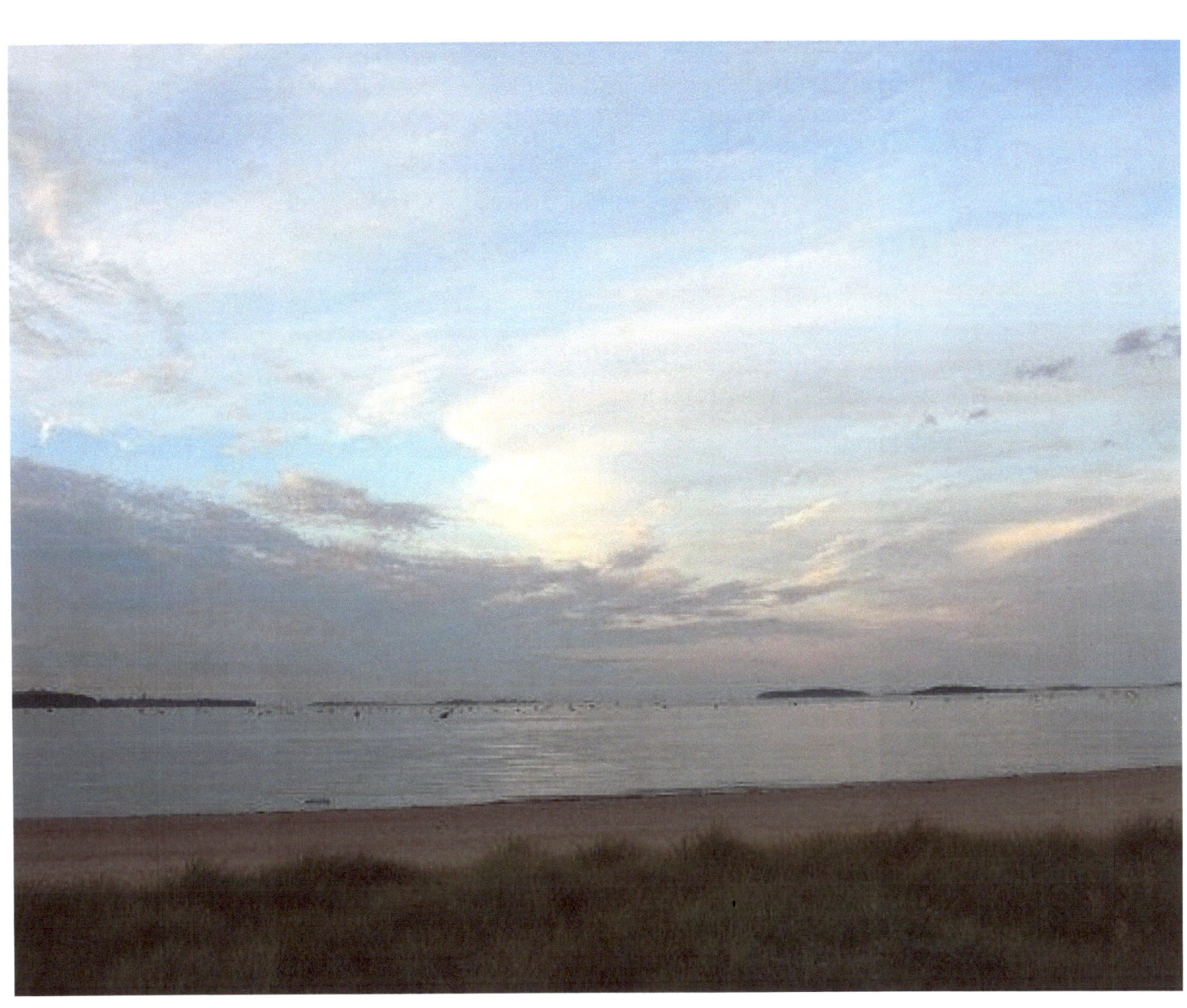

WACHUSETT I

WORCESTER, MASSACHUSETTS, USA

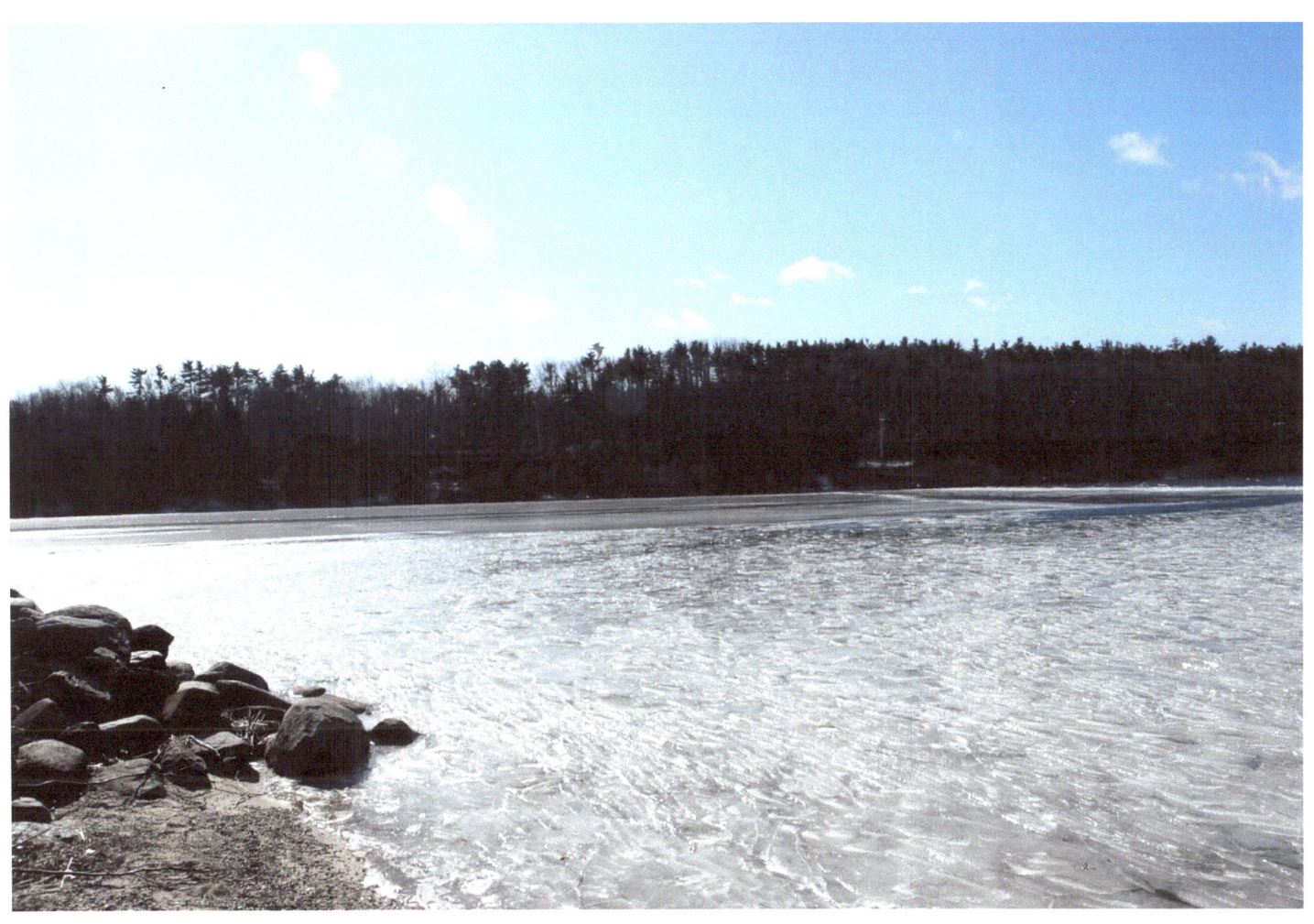

WACHUSETT II

WORCESTER, MASSACHUSETTS, USA

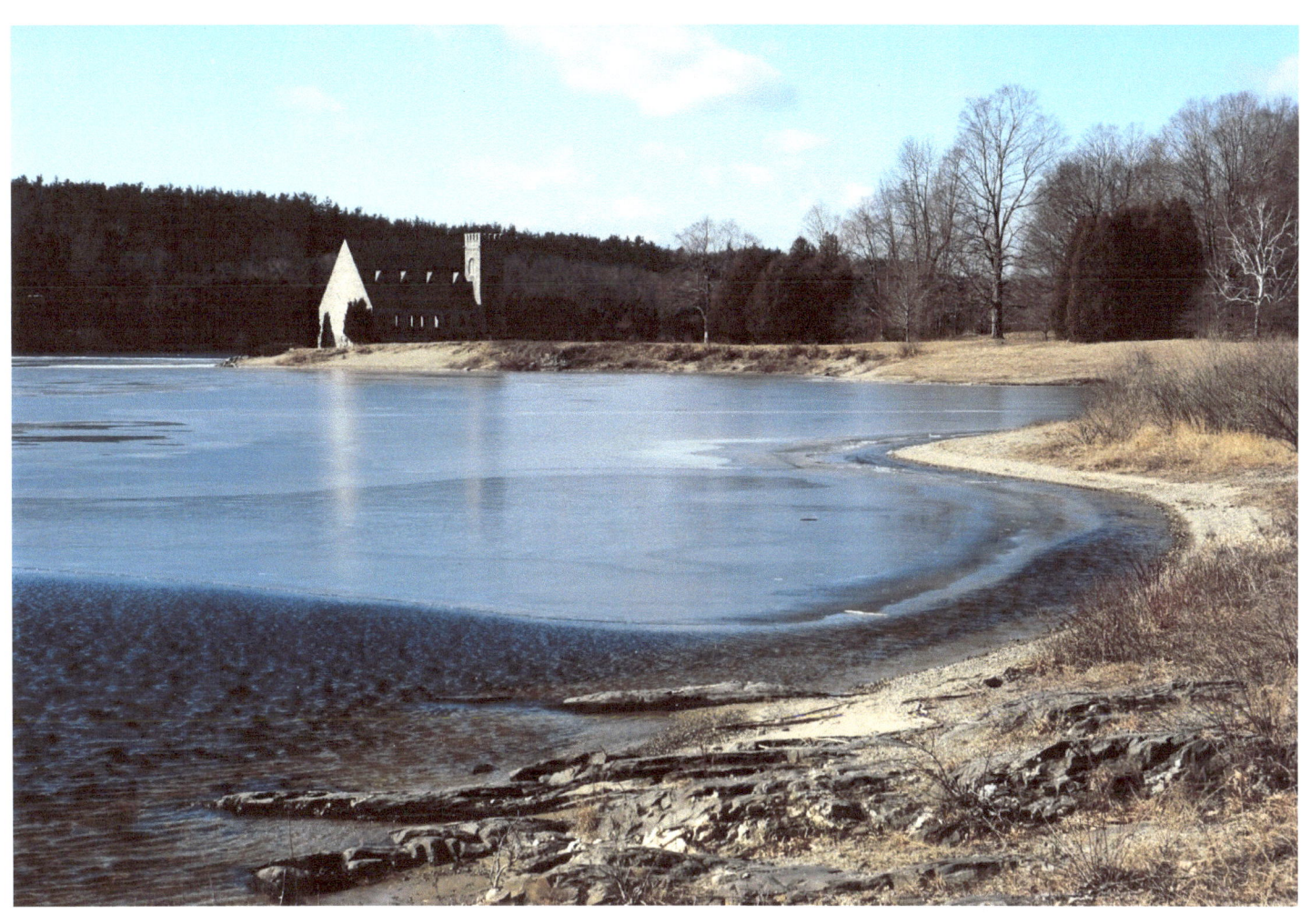

WACHUSETT III

WORCESTER, MASSACHUSETTS, USA

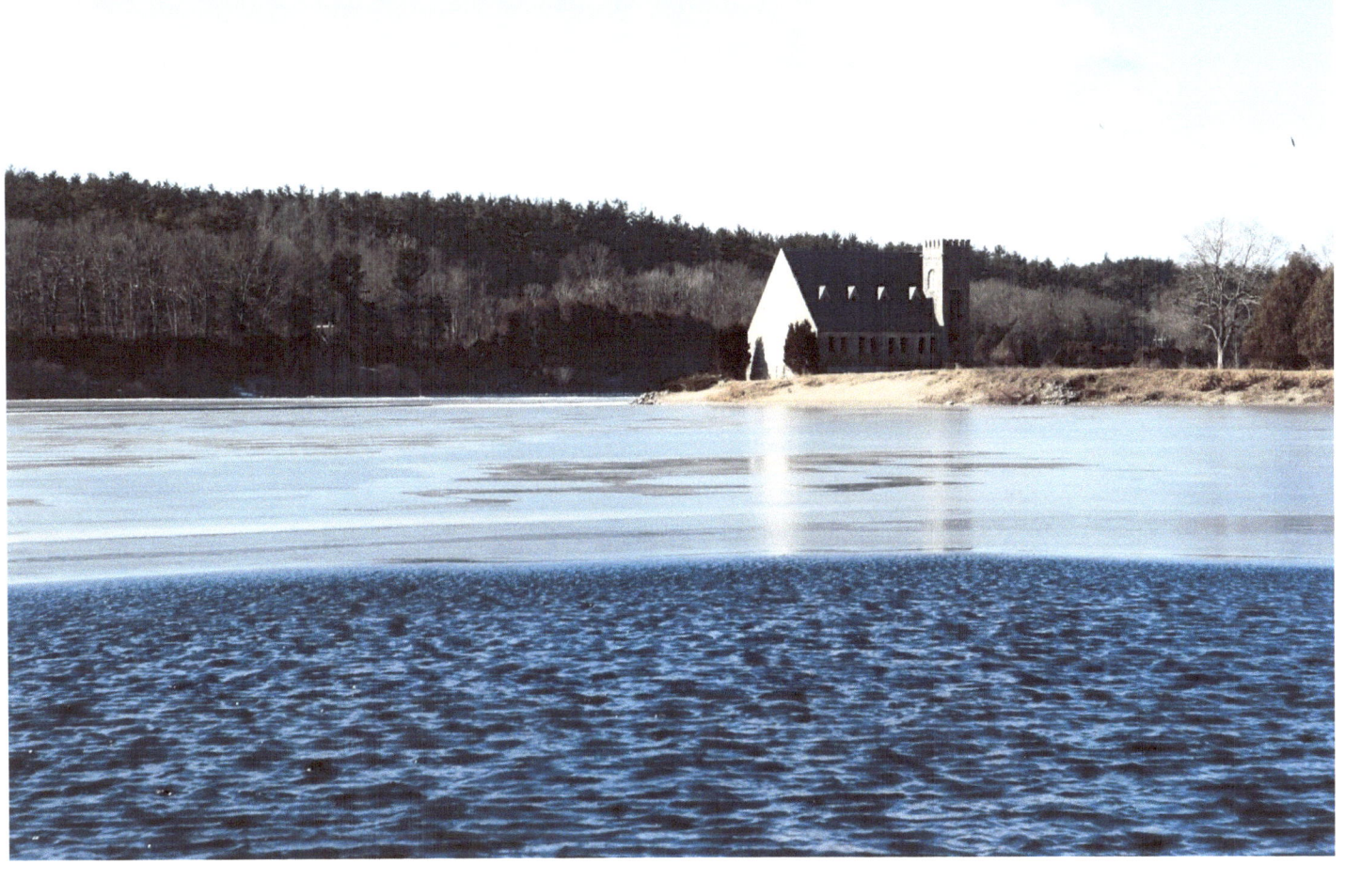

WACHUSETT IV

WORCESTER, MASSACHUSETTS, USA

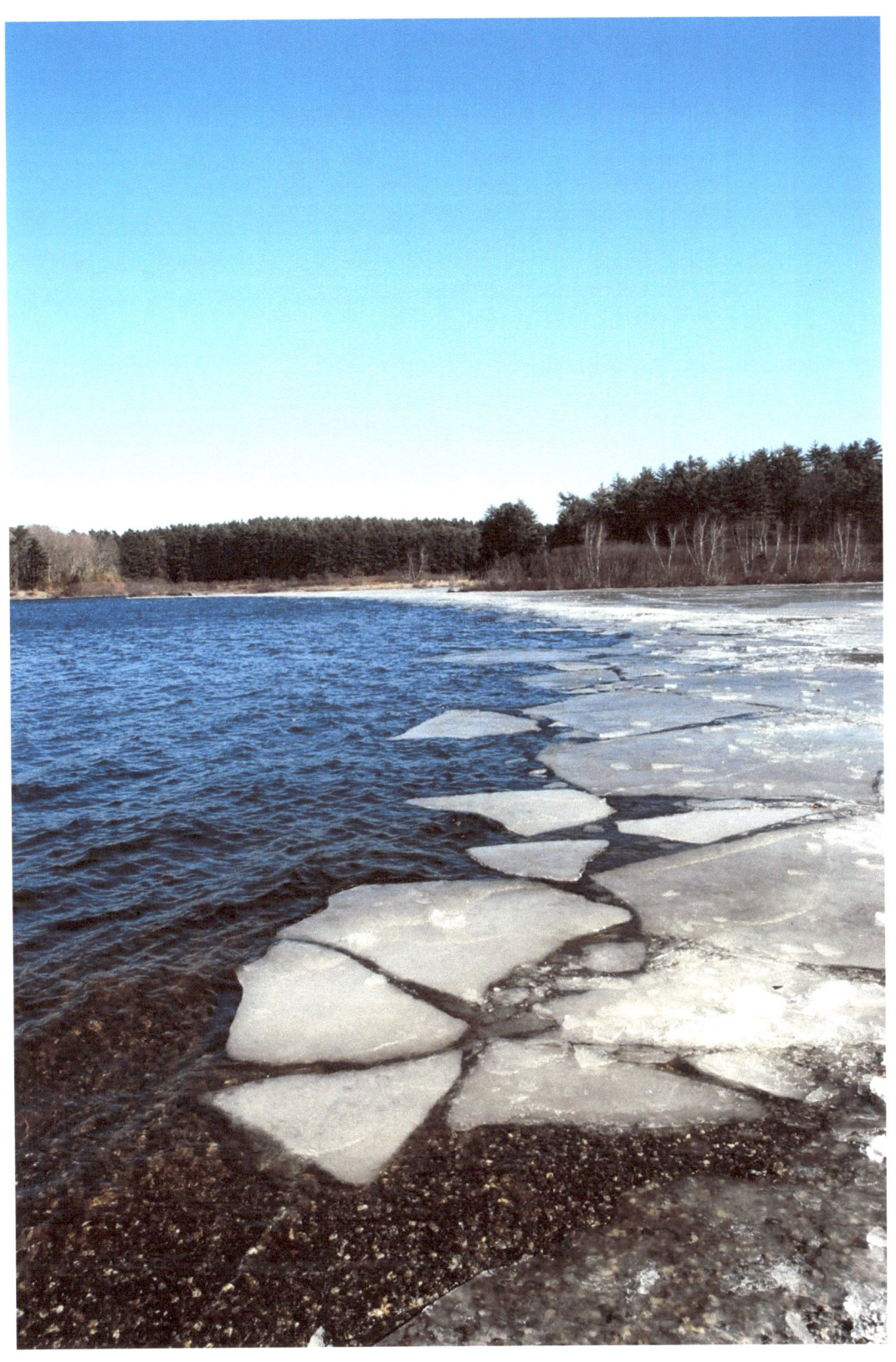

6 LOCATION-SHOOTS OUTSIDE OF MASSACHUSETTS:

I - NIAGARA FALLS, NY, USA

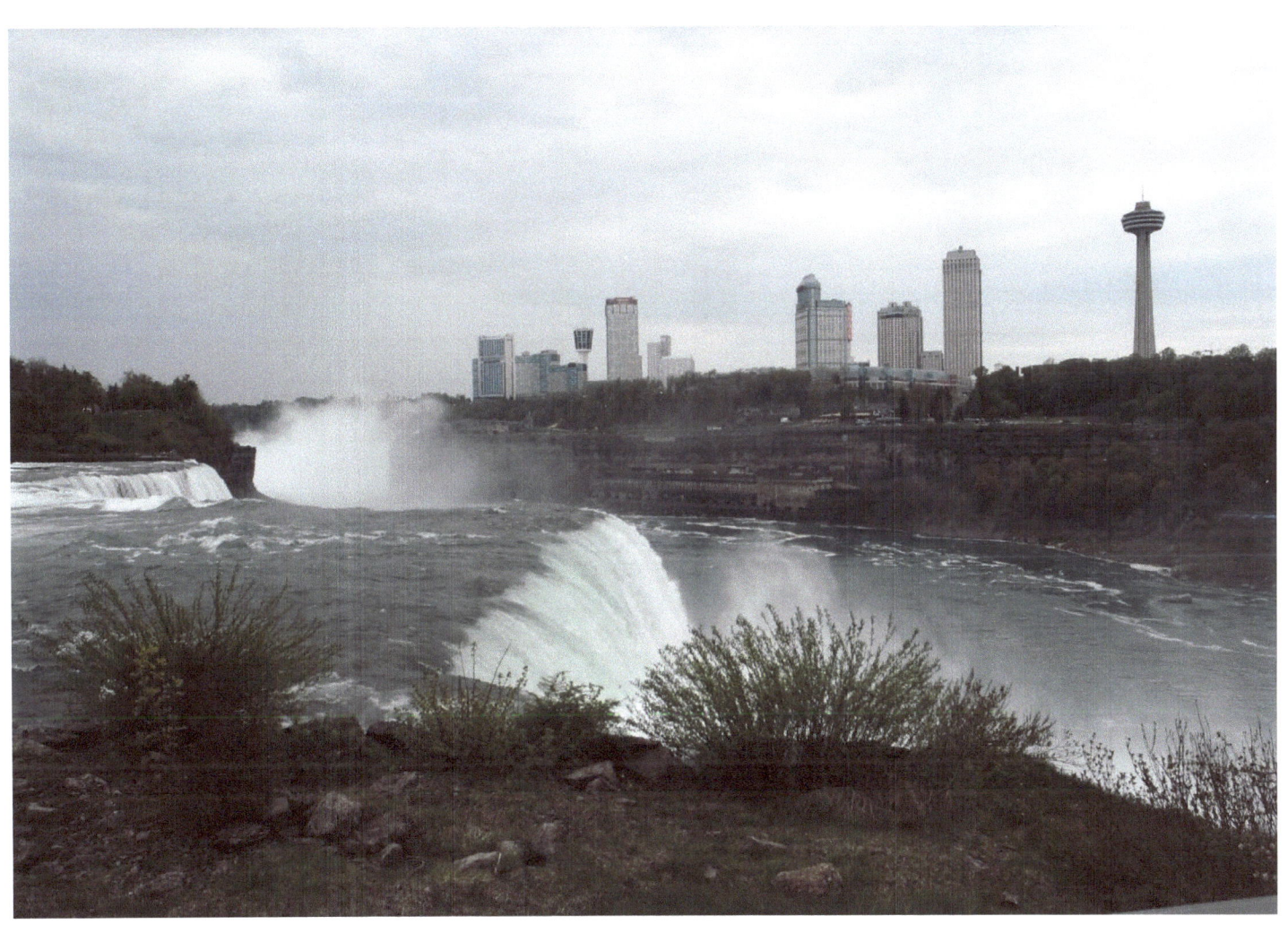

6 *LOCATION-SHOOTS OUTSIDE OF MASSACHUSETTS:*

II - ROUTE 80, PA, USA

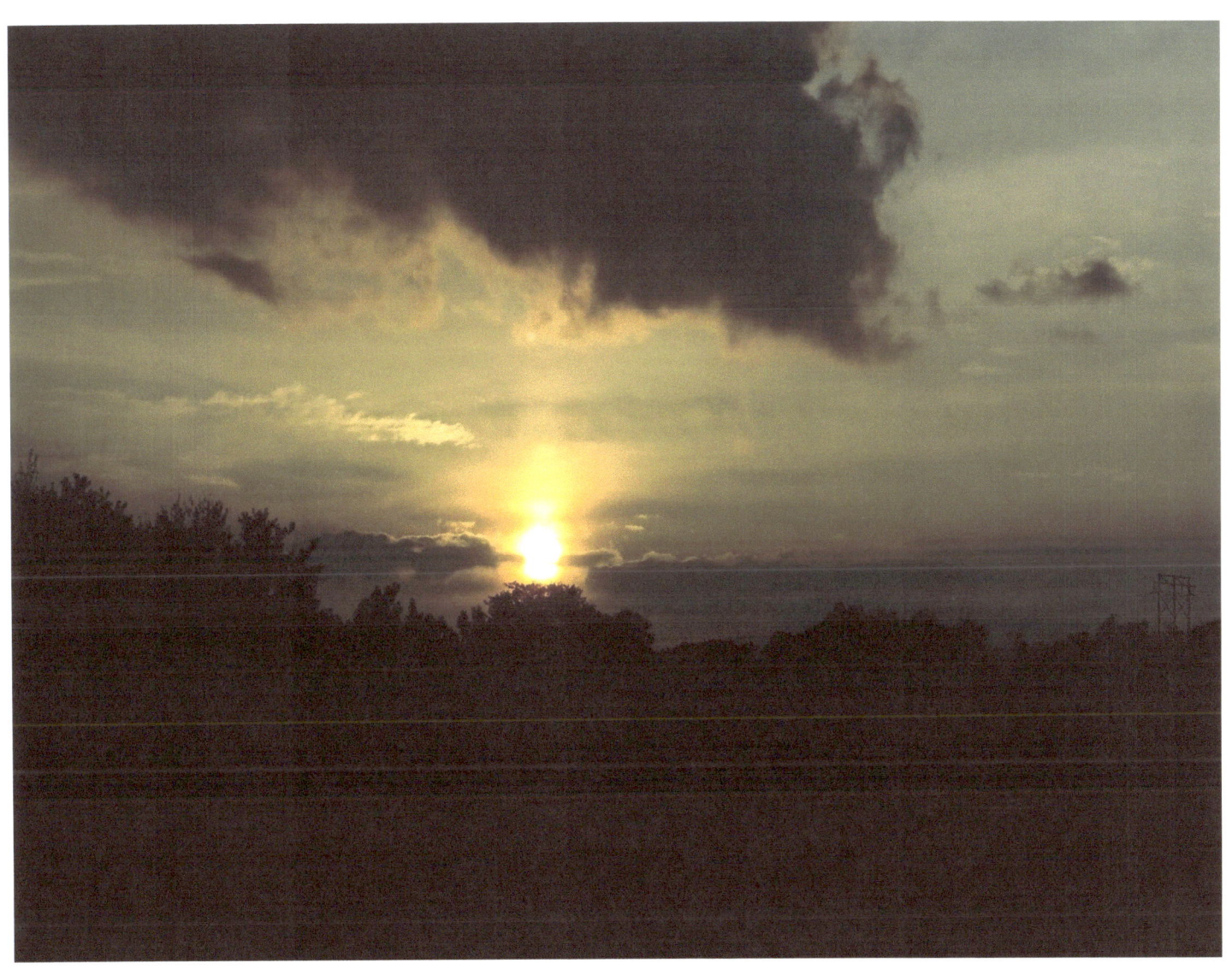

6 LOCATION-SHOOTS OUTSIDE OF MASSACHUSETTS:

III - LAKE CHAMPLAIN, VERMONT, USA

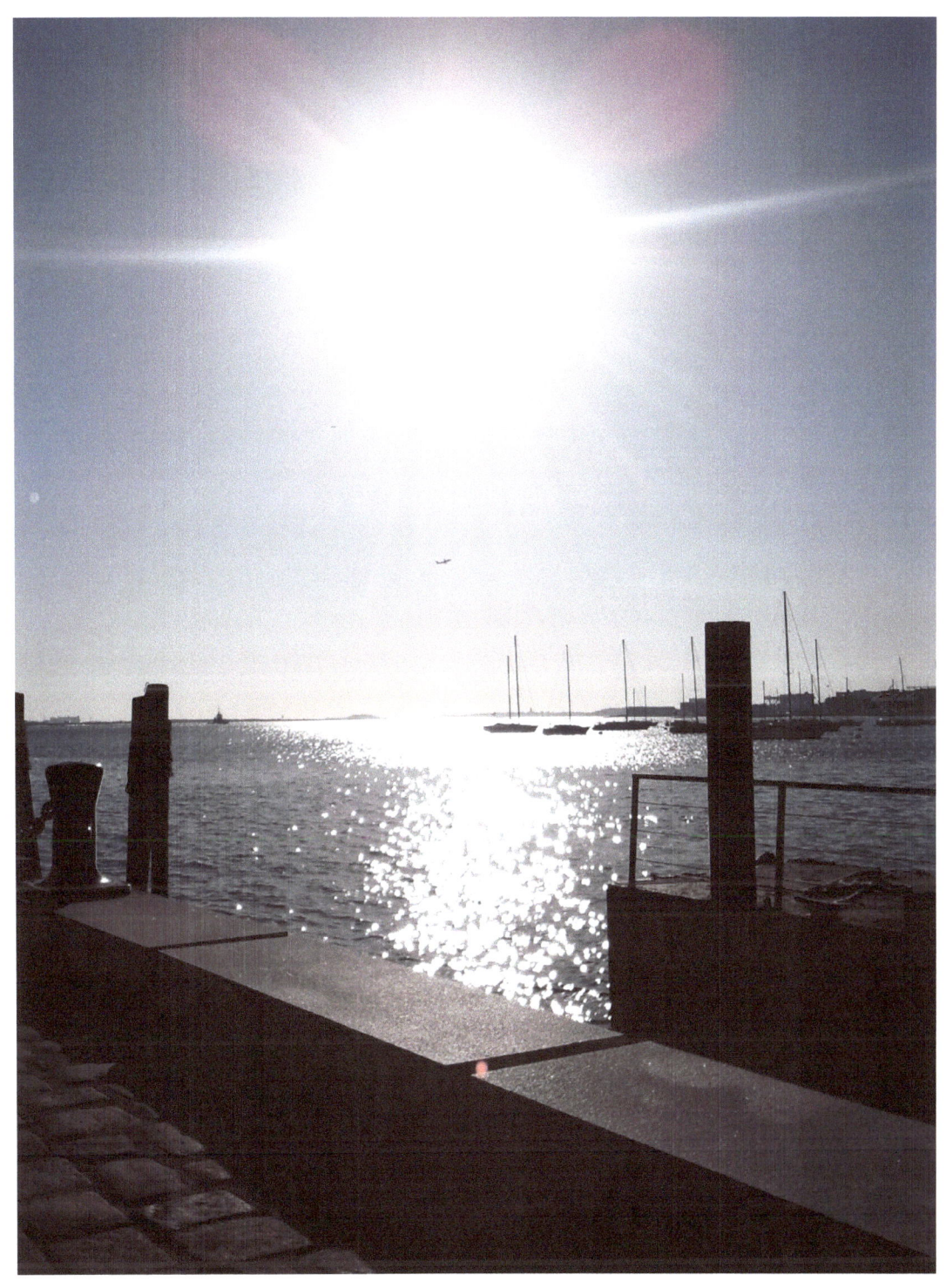

6 LOCATION-SHOOTS OUTSIDE OF MASSACHUSETTS:

IV - DE WALLEN, AMSTERDAM, NETHERLANDS

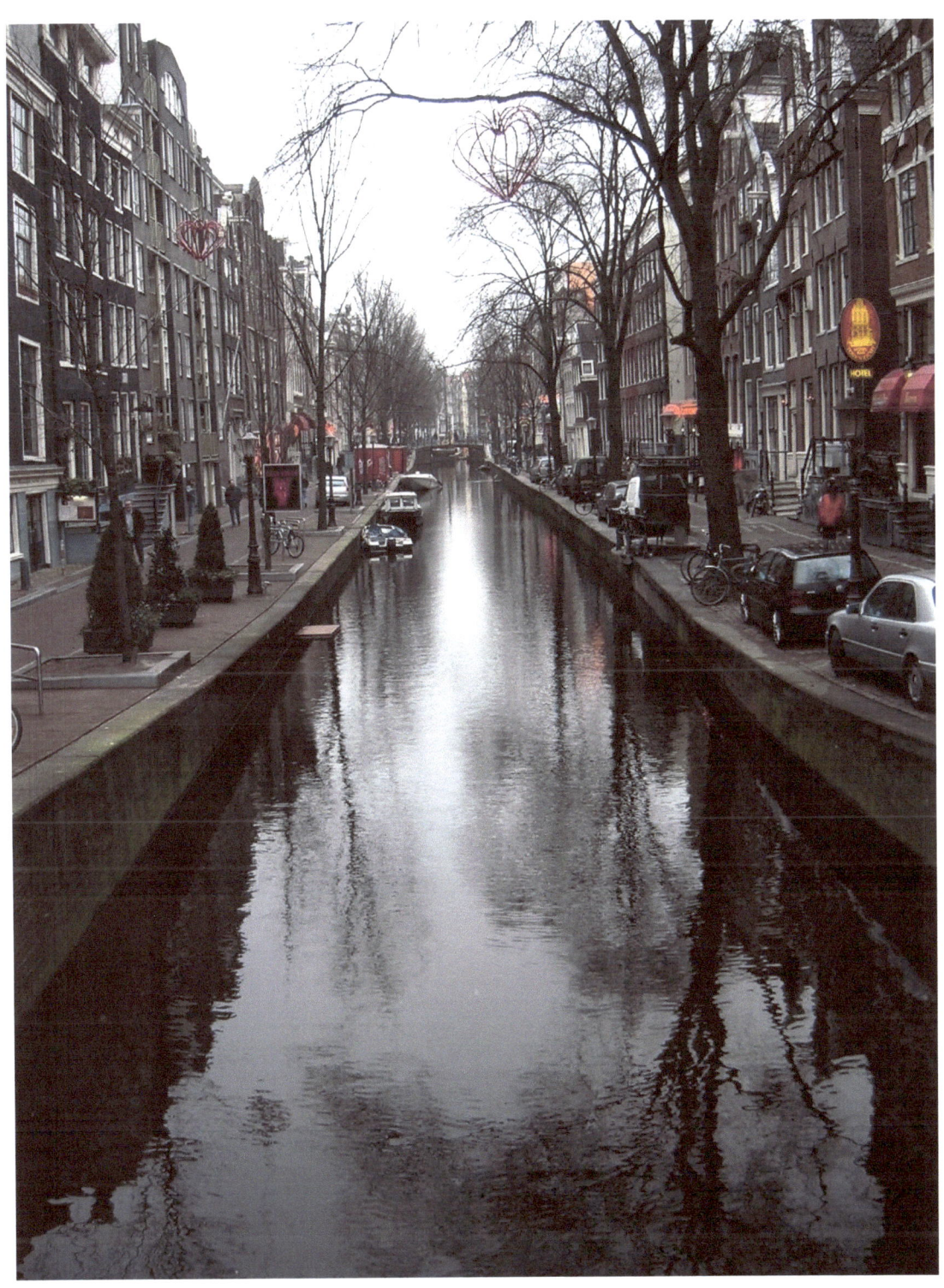

6 LOCATION-SHOOTS OUTSIDE OF MASSACHUSETTS:

V - PUNTA NIZUC, CANCUN, MEXICO

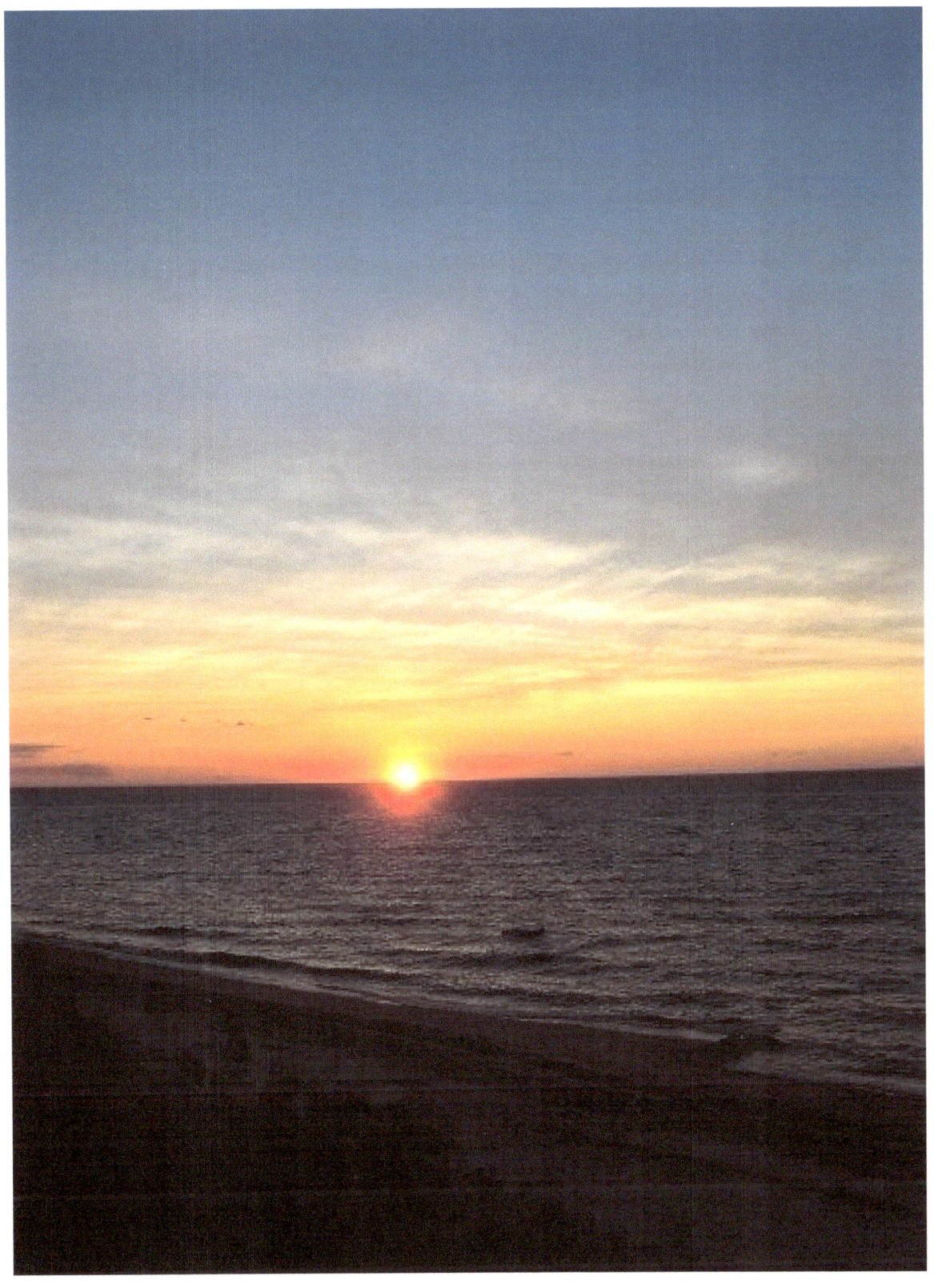

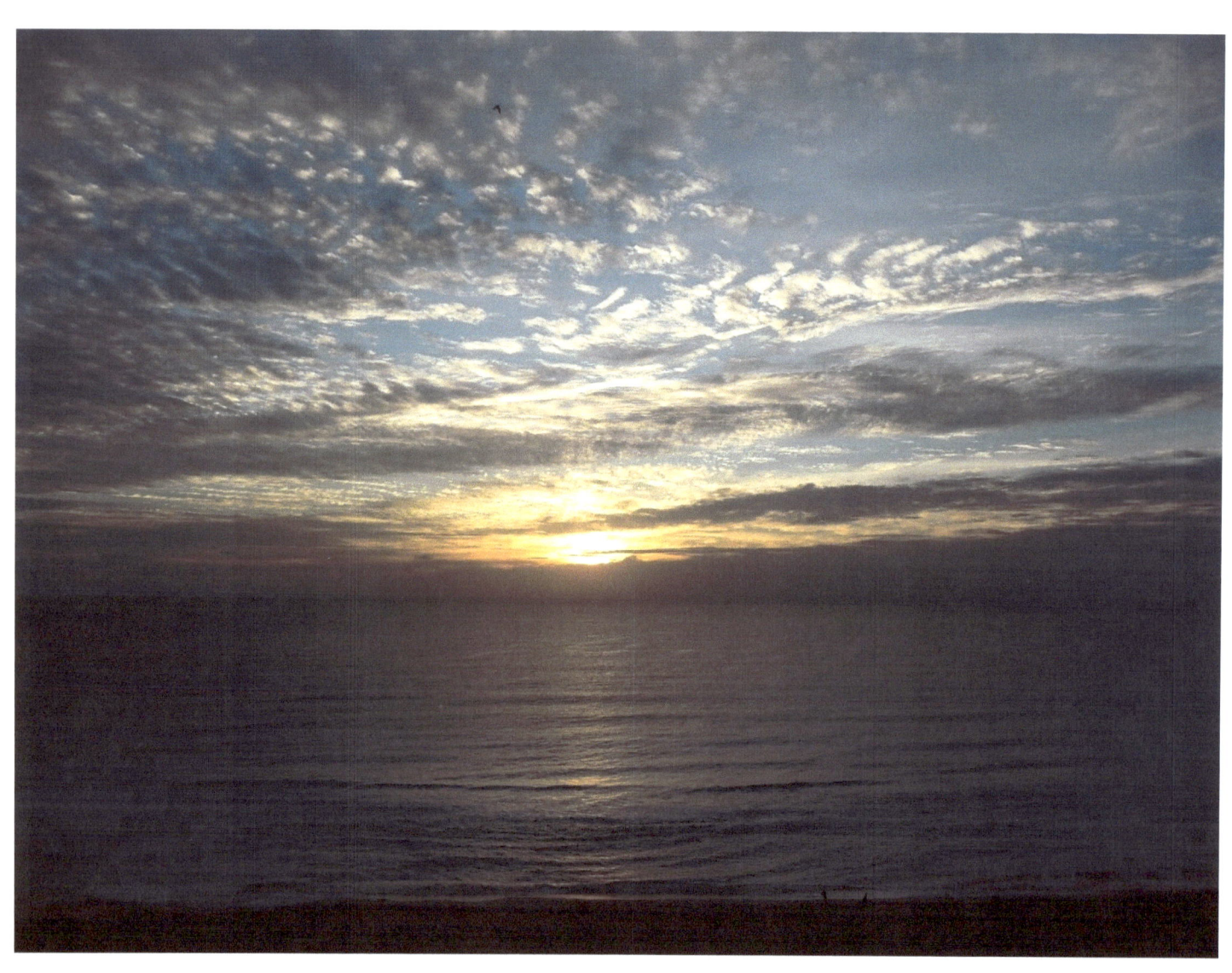

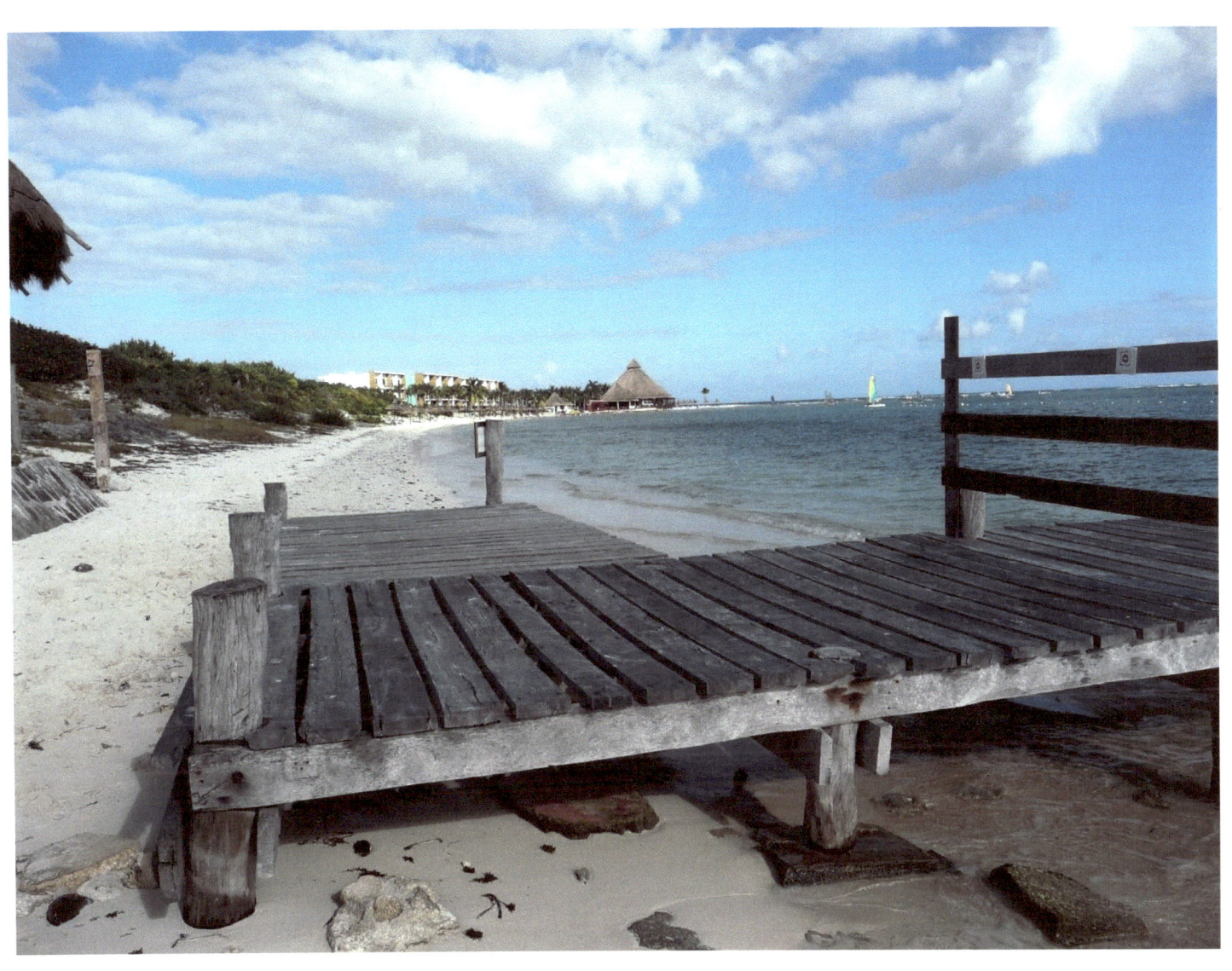

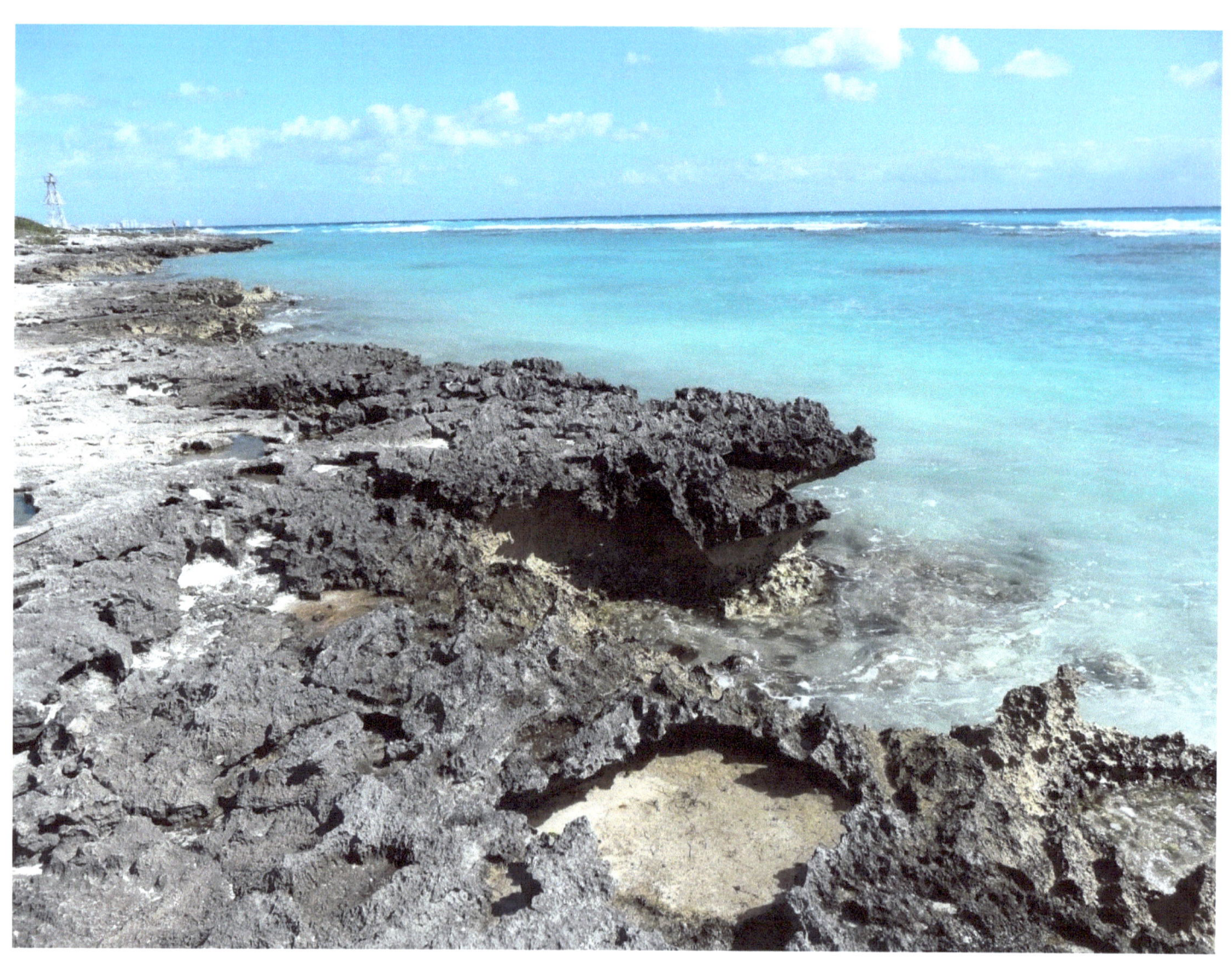

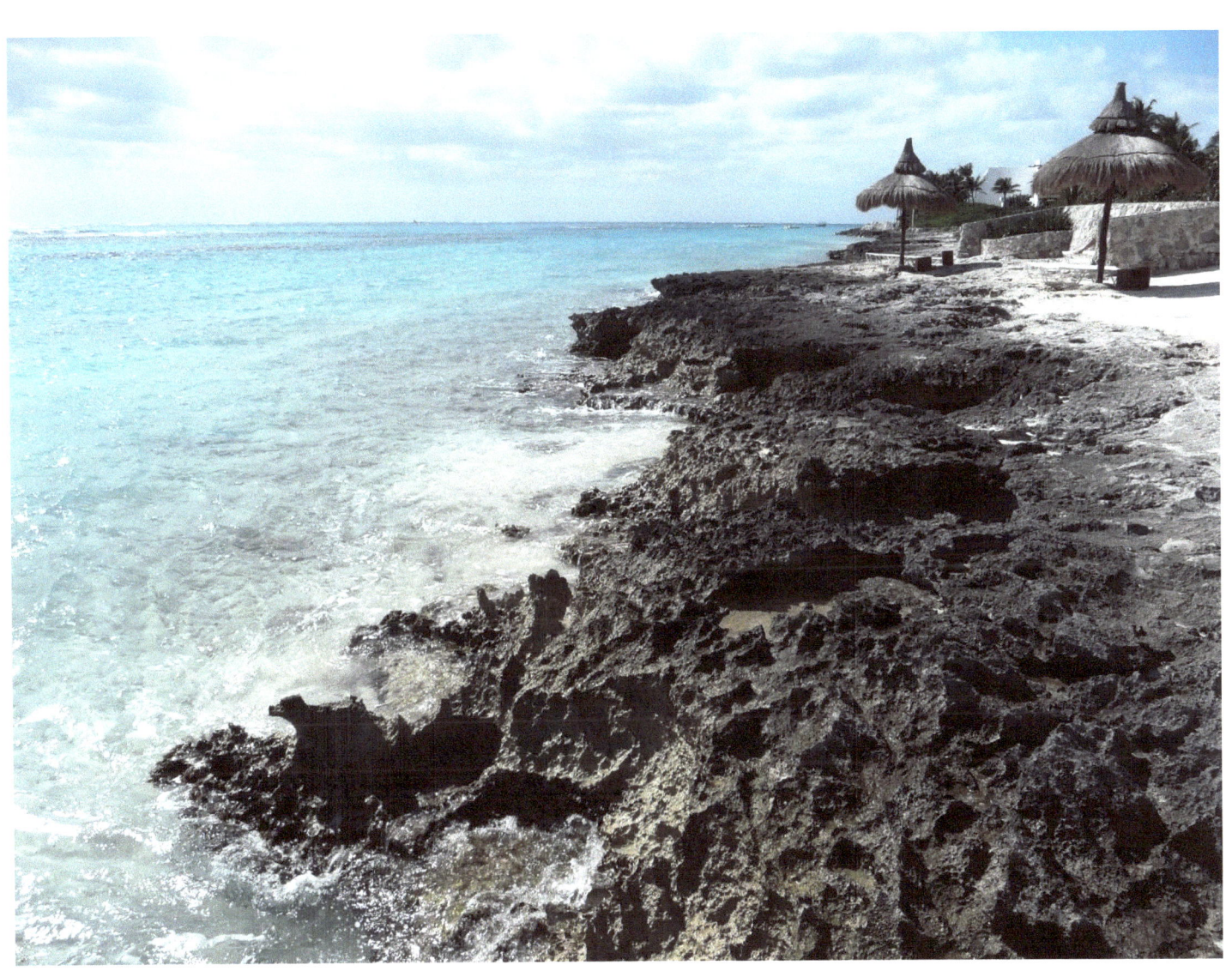

6 LOCATION-SHOOTS OUTSIDE OF MASSACHUSETTS:

VI - THAMES RIVER, LONDON, ENGLAND

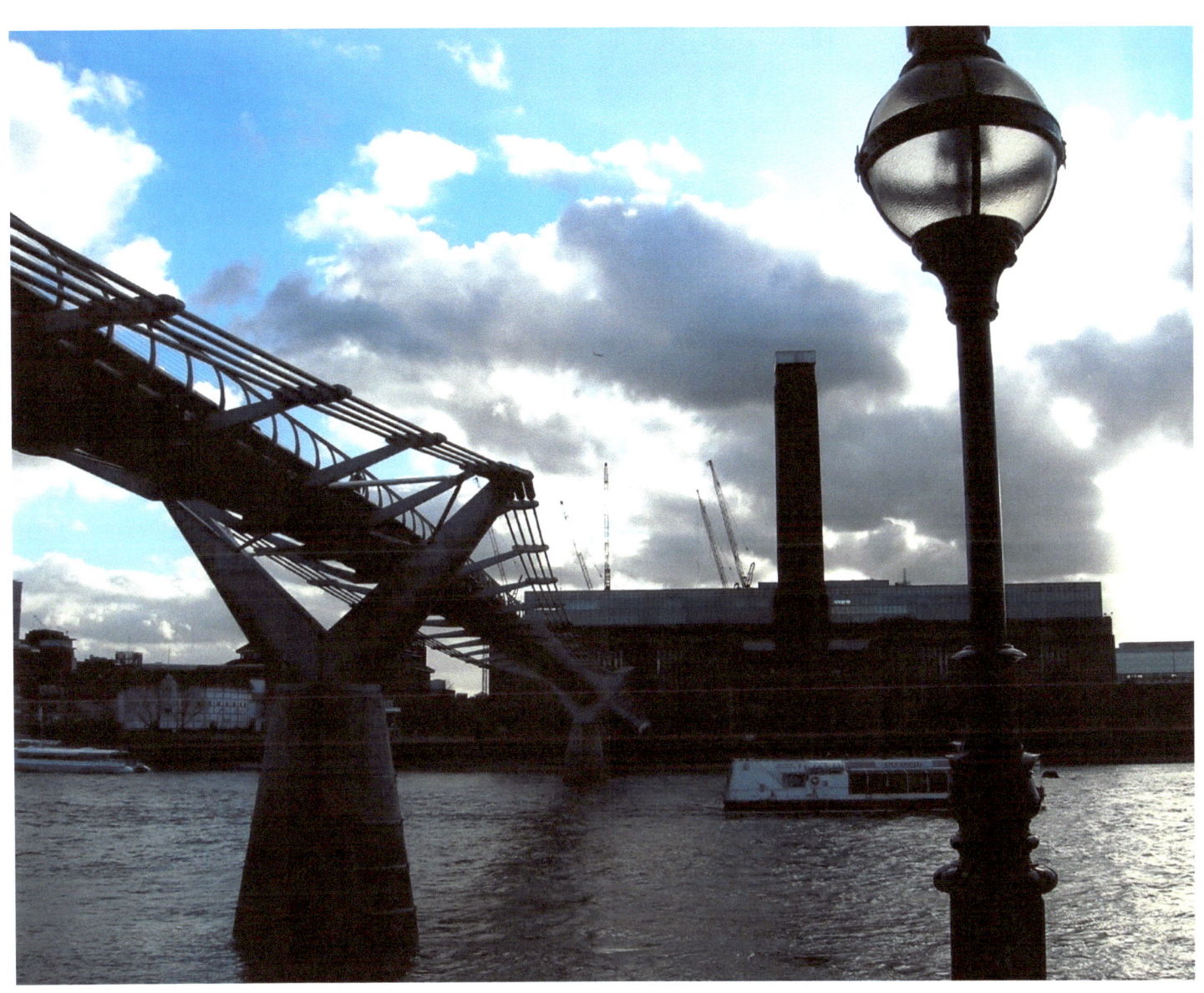

HIGH SCHOOL BLACK AND WHITE I

DOVER, MASSACHUSETTS, USA

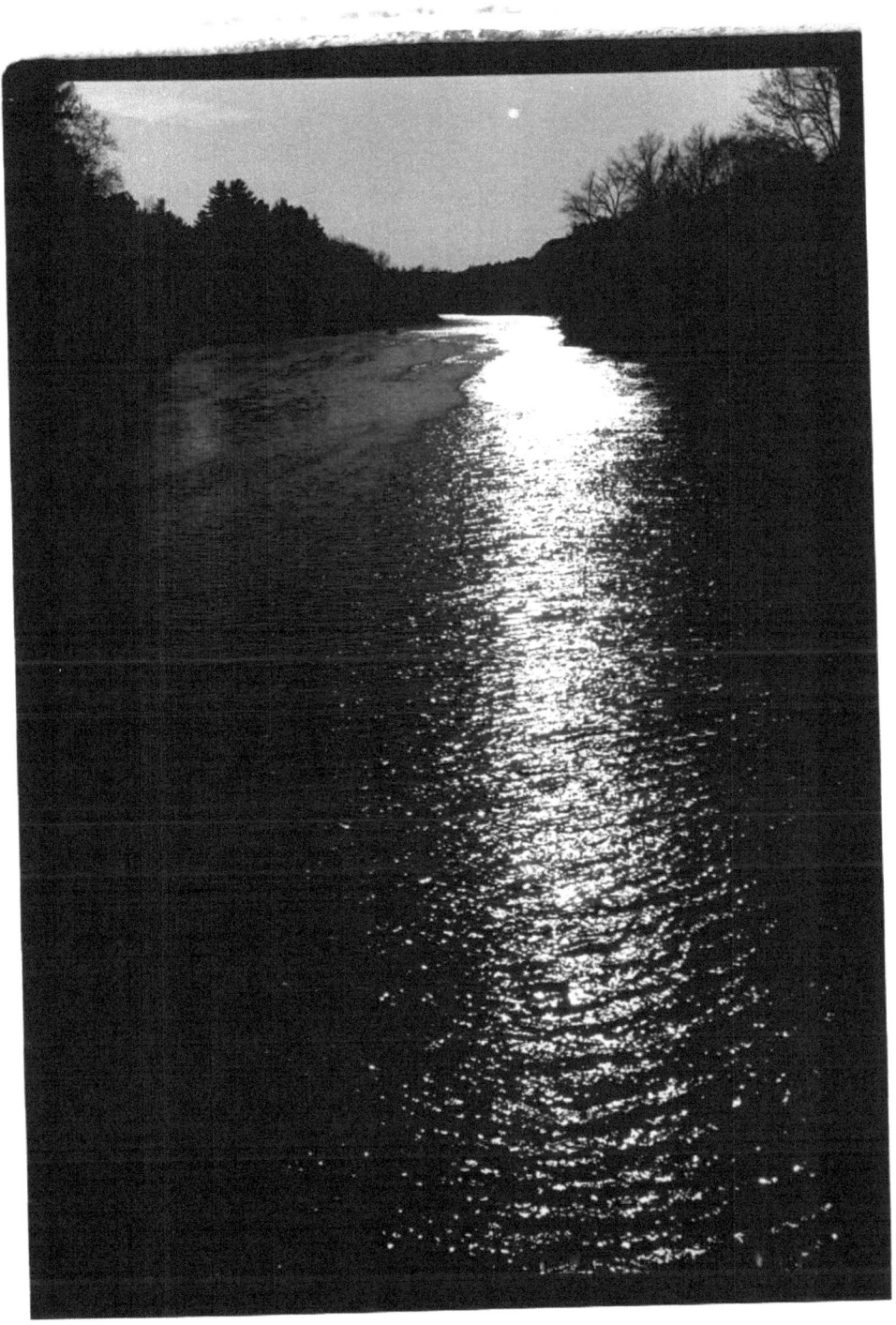

HIGH SCHOOL BLACK AND WHITE II

DOVER, MASSACHUSETTS, USA

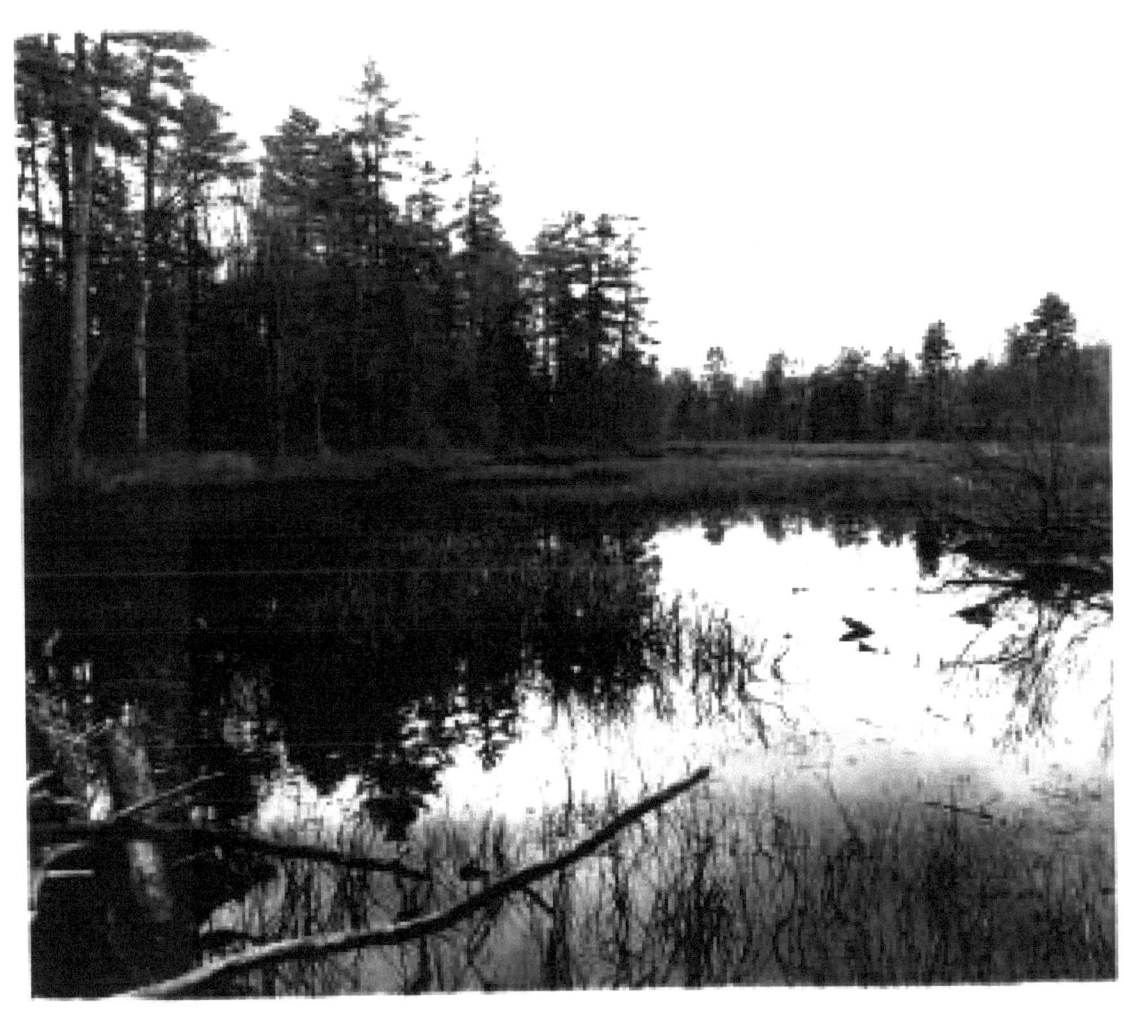

HIGH SCHOOL BLACK AND WHITE III

DOVER, MASSACHUSETTS, USA

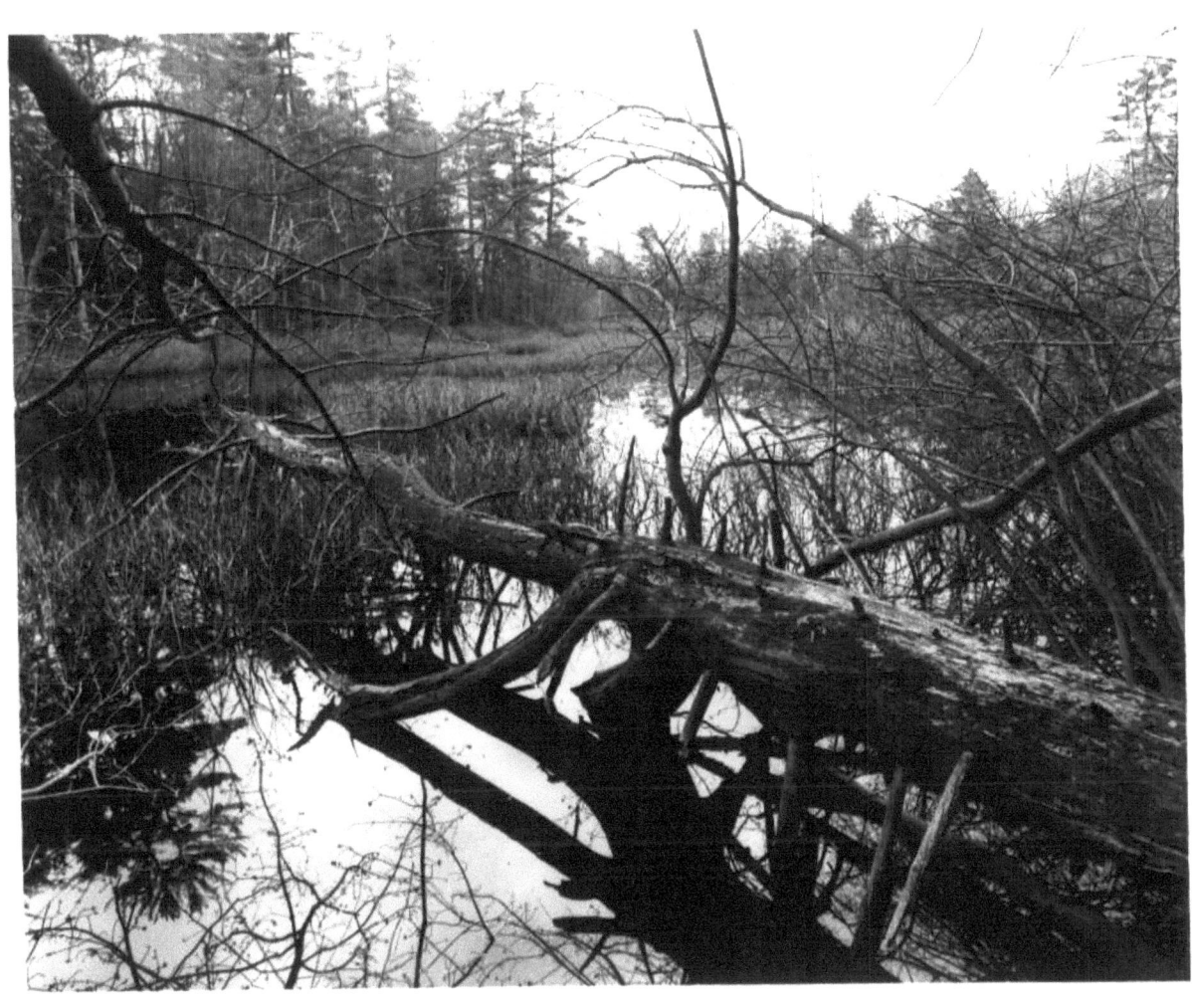

HIGH SCHOOL BLACK AND WHITE IV

DOVER, MASSACHUSETTS, USA

"THE SWAN"

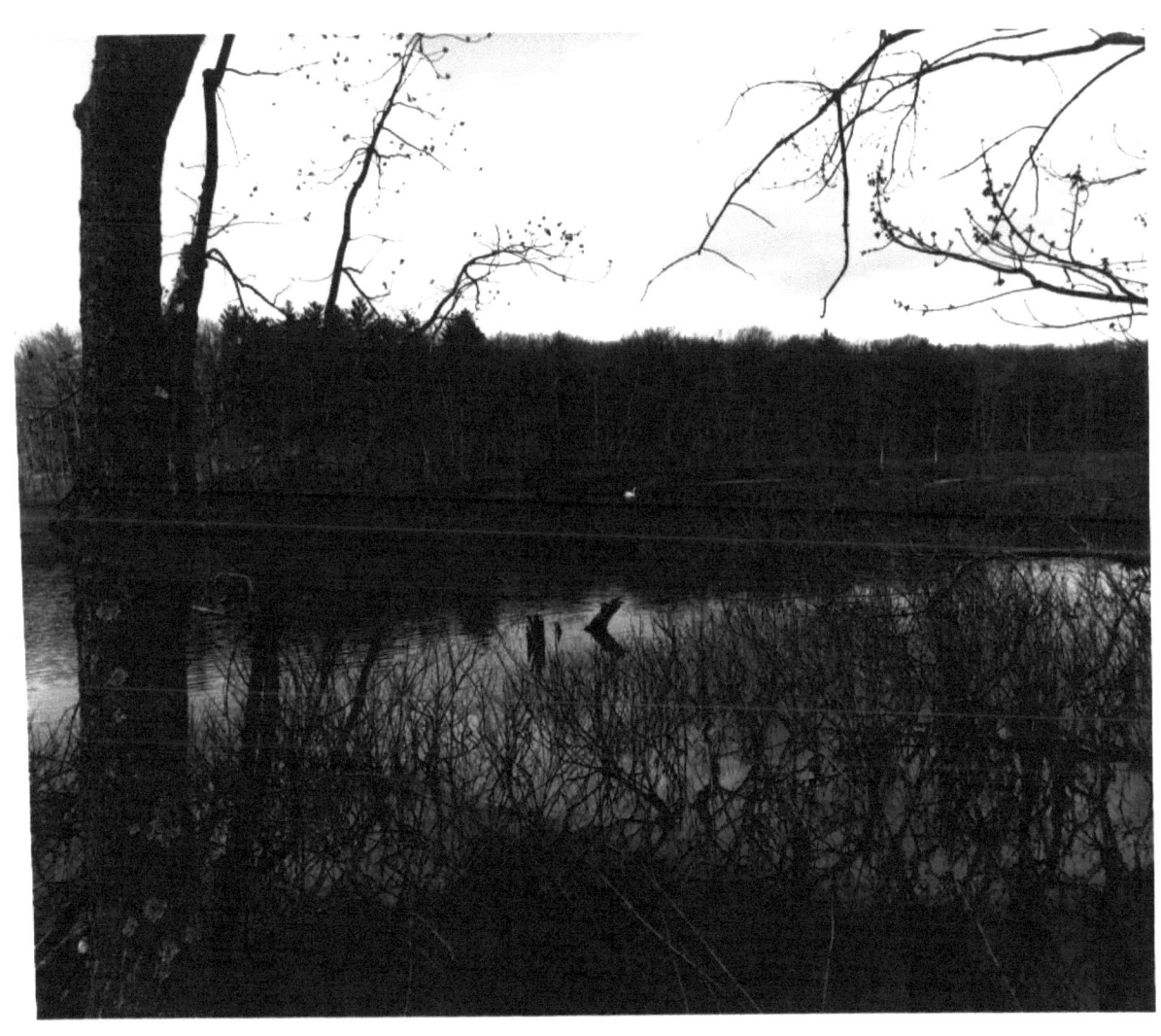

HIGH SCHOOL BLACK AND WHITE V

MONTICELLO, VIRGINIA, USA

"THE GUIDE TOLD OUR PARTY THAT THIS WAS AN ACTUAL STREAM THAT THOMAS JEFFERSON DRANK FROM ON HIS HORSE RIDES AROUND HIS ESTATE" - PETER

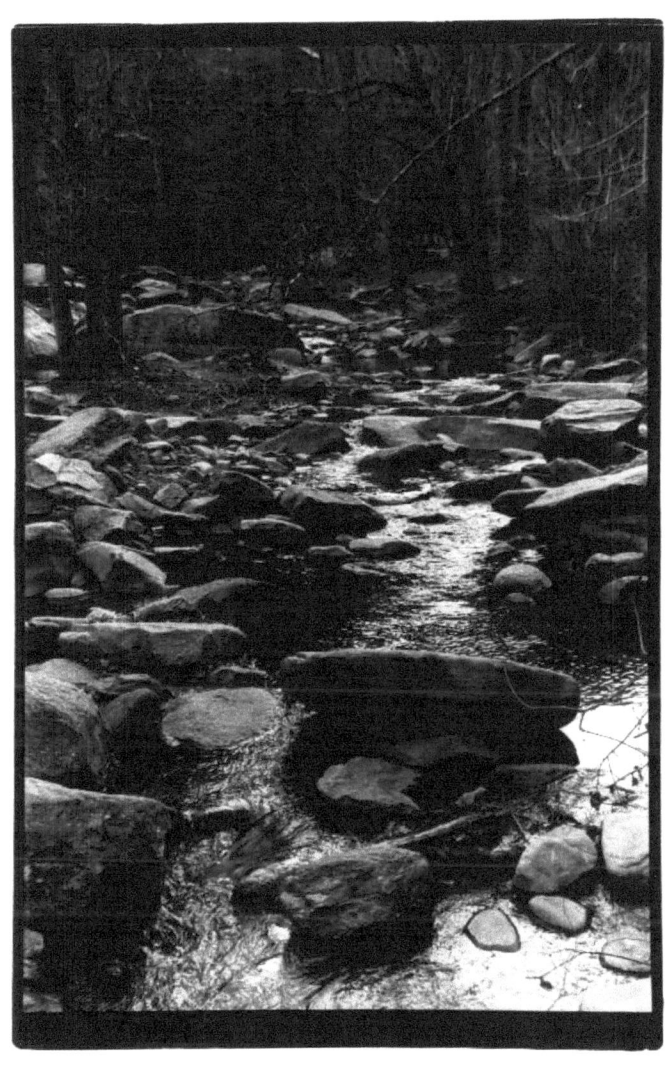